Counterpunch

Fred Smeijers

Counterpunch

making type in the sixteenth century,
designing typefaces now

Hyphen Press . London

First published by Hyphen Press, London, in 1996
This second edition published by Hyphen Press, London, in 2011

Author's text and drawings copyright © Fred Smeijers, 1996, 2011
Fournier translation copyright © estate of Harry Carter, 1930, 1973

The book was designed, typeset & made into pages in Adobe InDesign
by Corina Cotorobai, Antwerp. The text was set in the typeface Haultin,
designed by Fred Smeijers, Antwerp. Proofs of the pages in progress
were read by Eric Kindel, Reading. The book was made and printed
in Belgium by Drukkerij Schaubroeck, Nazareth

ISBN 978-0-907259-42-8

www.hyphenpress.co.uk

Voor mijn vader
and for past and present colleagues who share their knowledge

Contents

To the future

Appendices

Preface & acknowledgements

It seems that anything is possible now. We experience a world in which time, distance, and production circumstances hardly seem important any more. But for this very reason, we need to look back and talk with our predecessors. The way to do this is by doing what they have done. Only then is there a chance of thinking the way they thought. And then there is some basis for comparison. When you stand on common ground with your predecessors, you can define your own position, estimate progress or see what has been forgotten in the meantime. Talking like this with colleagues from the past has nothing to do with sentimentality or nostalgia or a useless search for craftsmanship. It has however everything to do with bringing back knowledge that can serve as a mirror for ourselves and our technical achievements. An honest assessment of this kind is thus an essential step in the search for relevant improvement: now, and for the future.

This book does not try to put history into perfect order. It is not concerned to list all the facts. Rather, it tries to look through and beyond these historical particulars, to be able to see what is fundamental and of enduring relevance. So this book is written not for historians – though it would certainly not hurt them to read it – but for the makers and users of type. I hope it will be understandable to anyone interested in type, and not just type designers and traditionally oriented typographers. Some pages here might even be useful to the vast numbers of people who are not graphic designers at all, but who find themselves doing typography on the personal computer and laser printer.

The first chapters of this work deal with general considerations in typography and in thinking about letters. Then it gets on to history. Some of this material can be found in other books too. But here there is a description of how the French and the Flemish punchcutters worked in the period 1520–1600, and why they did it that way. The book draws some lessons from the practice of punchcutting, and goes on to look

9

at some present issues in designing type. Finally, conclusions are drawn about what our technical liberation has really achieved, so far.

In making this second edition of the book I have resisted the temptation to incorporate all that I have learned about sixteenth-century punches in the years since 1996, when the first edition was published. Only necessary corrections and updatings have been made, including the addition of some new pictures. But we have reset the whole book, and in a new typeface.

Of the people who have supported this project, I want first, and most, to thank my editor, Robin Kinross. Without his initiative, trust, and above all, patience, the book would never have reached publication. Among those who collaborated on making the first edition, most essential were Françoise Berserik and Peter Paul Kloosterman. Important help also came from Luce van Alphen, Erik van Blokland, Jelle Bosma, Matthew Carter, Jane Howard, Josée Langen, Mathieu Lommen, Martin Majoor, James Mosley, the late Paul Stiff, Erik Vos, Margreet Windhorst. Henk Drost and Christian Paput generously provided detailed information about the traditions of punchcutting. In correcting the text for the second edition, John Downer's comments were valuable. This new edition has been designed and typeset by Corina Cotorobai, whose hard work and gentle pressure turned idea into reality.

For permission to reproduce material: I especially thank Matthew Carter, for allowing me to reprint passages from the edition of Fournier, translated and edited by his father, Harry Carter. Other acknowledgements are made on pages 196–7, where exact sources of illustrations are also given. Last but not least, I am grateful to the Plantin-Moretus Museum, not just for permission to reproduce material in its possession, but as the welcoming home for much of the historical research for this book.

FS, Antwerp, June 2011

Fundamental factors

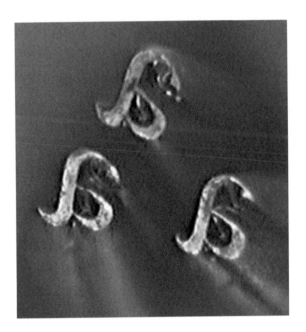

These three lowercase a's belong to one set of punches. Why would the punchcut-
ter make three of them? Maybe because this is a weak punch that breaks easily?
I do not think so. The lowercase i, for example, is much weaker: because of the
dot that tends to break off when hitting a strike. And we do not find an i twice in
any historical set. I think the reason could be this: the punchcutter just liked to
make these a's. Just as these days a young type designer might love to draw an a
in idle moments: when waiting for a print, or during a long conversation on the
telephone. The maker of these three punches then could not decide which one was
best. So why not include all three of them?

1 Why this book?

The origins of this book lie in the years that I worked as a typographer with the research & development department of Océ. In the mid-1980s, this giant Dutch photocopier firm independently developed a mid-volume laser printer. And then Océ began to realize – in common with other firms – that the main product of this machine would be office documents typeset in monospaced and also typographic fonts. But they, like so many other manufacturers, had hardly any typographic knowledge or awareness. Typographically skilled people were soon persuaded to work for them.

In the early days of personal computers and office automation, Océ seemed an interesting place at which to work. It was however also a difficult place at which to work, because of the demands of the technically oriented people there. It was a part of my task to reduce the rift between technicians and the type specialists. Technicians tend to think only in numbers; graphic designers tend to think only in visual forms and colours. There were often clashes and breakdowns in communication between the two kinds of people. The technical people used to ask questions such as: 'Why is 300 dots-per-inch not enough to print Times italic? Why are those serifs and hairlines that thin. It is ridiculous!' Or: 'A character is a black shape, right? So why, at a resolution of 300 dpi, is the white space between characters suddenly so important?'

I heard such questions over and over again. It drove me mad with frustration. I could find no adequate explanations. The answers given by my designer colleagues usually derived from a hostile attitude towards the apparently silly questions asked by the engineers. But the questions are not silly: from an engineer's point of view, they are quite understandable. The designers' point of view is also understandable, given their education and assumptions. When you realize that you cannot answer simple and basic questions about your work – that's hard to swallow. And certainly when it is an engineer who made you realize this.

I decided to look for answers. The books gave hardly any. What to do? Start right at the beginning. Not everything about type can be explained by knowledge of the broad-nib pen. After writing, chiselling, scratching and drawing, came punchcutting. But I had never seen a real punch. I was living in Eindhoven: the Plantin-Moretus Museum in Antwerp was just an hour away. And I knew I could see some punches there. Punchcutting was the technique responsible for 450 years of typographic letterforms. The Plantin Museum – in 2005 named by UNESCO as a 'World Heritage Site' – has by far the largest collection of punches, matrices, and related documents that survive from the sixteenth century: thus, the oldest typographic materials at our disposal. Besides that, handcut type has often been used as a reference when a design has been translated to a new typesetting technique. The letterpress-printed image is certainly a good reference when one is working on a design that has been used for long time in metal. To get a better view of the problems that were typical of what was then the current technology, it seemed wise to know as much as possible about the technique that lies behind our reference. As my head was hovering for the first time above the showcases of the Plantin Museum, I thought: is that all? Is that what all the mystery is about? Is this such a difficult task to perform? No, I do not believe that. Metal is a material that requires great patience. It may take a long time, but it cannot be difficult. Let's try, and see what happens.

So I started to cut punches on my own. The first attempts could not have been more discouraging. My respect for the contents of the Plantin Museum went up by the minute. After some time I realized that I could not do it: not today, not tomorrow. The only thing to do was to ask for help from my father: a man put into a machine-tool factory at the age of 14, just after the Second World War, in order to play his role in rebuilding society. For as long as I have known him, there has never been anything that he could not make, repair or explain – if it concerned metal and mechanics. In the end I persuaded him to come with me to the Plantin Museum.

My father was, however, absolutely unimpressed by the punches. Things got worse when I told him that they were made around 1560, and that still no one really knows how they were made, or how to recreate them today. He started to laugh. He had to admit that the people who made these antiques must have been good craftsmen, no doubt about that. To claim, however, that this could not be done today was absolutely untrue. He said that if I wanted punches, he knew at least a dozen people who could do this, including himself. He said that he had made numerous punches or punch-like things in his life. For example, die-cutting knives for cigar bands. Very often they had these nasty little curls and little pointed tips. As he said this he pointed to a punch in the case. It was a roman lowercase r. What my father saw had of course nothing to do with type; it arose out of a technical problem. This is always the case with punchcutting. It became clear that, in the first place, it was just a matter of technical and manual dexterity.

This short visit was a good thing. My father started to talk about steel and what you could do with it: tempering, hardening, to various degrees. He told me about counterpunches and how to strike them. He told me about files, gravers, and how to make them. He told me about cutting angles. He told me all about dexterity. Yet he had never cut type.

Now I had really started. Progress in cutting punches began to come quickly. After I had made some punches with an x-height of about two millimetres, I decided to take to Océ's photographic department some of the tiny curls of steel, which are made as one pushes a graver along a punch to refine the image. Some electron-microscope pictures and measurements were made. The results were, of course, just numbers expressing the size and thickness of these tiny little curls. But these numbers, together with a little typographic history, answered some of the engineers' questions. They gave much clearer information than any book could do.

2 Terminology

The more technical terms used in the book are explained as they occur. The meanings of other terms such as 'serif' or 'lowercase' can be found in any dictionary, and it would be pedantic to repeat definitions here. But there are some general English-language typographic words and concepts that are often confusingly used, and I will explain here my understanding of them.

'Character' is the large term that includes the things we call a 'letter', a 'numeral', a punctuation mark, and all the other signs that one might find in a 'character set'. In the world of computing, 'character' means just code, and the black mark is a 'glyph'. But in this book, character means the visible sign. 'Figure' is another term for 'numeral'. In discussing the appearance of these marks, I have often used the words 'form' and 'shape', sometimes with a sense of some difference between the two, though that is very hard to pin down. 'Letterform' is a useful word, with a meaning that should be obvious.

I have used the words 'type' and 'typeface' rather than the now very common term 'font'. The meanings of these three words come from the processes that are a main subject of this book. In letterpress printing, a 'type' is a piece of metal, on one end of which – its face – there is the image of a character. The term 'font' refers to a set of types, unified by visual resemblance, at one size only. ('Font' was originally American-English, while in British-English it was 'fount'.) Punchcutters would cut a font of pica type. Even now one can buy a 'font' of 12 point type from one of the surviving metal foundries. This is the original sense of 'font' and I think it is better reserved for what it exactly describes.

A set of types over a whole range of sizes – a set of fonts – we call a 'typeface'. The idea of a typeface emerged only gradually. As is discussed in the book (chapter 20), in the sixteenth century – but not before – we begin to see fonts joined by a consistent, unifying notion of their forms. Later, the concept of a typeface became enlarged to include variant character sets: italic, small capitals, bold, light, and more. Around 1900, typefaces become commodities, with trade names to help identify and sell the product. 'Garamond' is a product of the twentieth century, not the sixteenth.

'Leading', like 'font', is a muddled hangover from metal technology. It does not describe anything very much. I have avoided the term, and used 'line increment' instead. This has the advantage of describing the distance between baselines of text: which is the dimension that is actually useful in specifying text composition.

Nederland & Europa

3.1

A quickly written but clear word which shows the significant parts of each letter formed by one stroke. For example: the first e is built up out of two strokes. Whereas the word 'land' is made out of just one stroke.

3.2

Two kinds of letter are shown here. The a is written: each significant part is made with one stroke. Writing is very direct, with no chance of correction. The g is drawn: built up out of numerous strokes made carefully next to each other. Drawing takes much more time, to consider and check the slowly growing form.

18

3 The three ways of making letters

There are just three kinds of letters: written, drawn or 'lettered', and typographic. They follow from and are defined by their method of production: writing; drawing or 'lettering'; and all the methods by which typographic letters are generated. The complications behind this strict division, particularly in the second category, will be explained in what follows.

Written letters can be used only during the process of writing itself: the moment of production and of use is one and the same. If I write some letters, make photocopies, then cut up and paste some of these letters together, then this process leaves writing behind, and becomes lettering. Writing only happens when you make letters with your hand (or another part of your body) and when every significant part of the letter is made in one stroke. In writing, whole letters, even whole words, can he made in one stroke [3.1, 3.2]. This process of writing is not limited to pen and paper. You can write with a brush on stone, or with a stick in sand on the beach, or, if need be, with the tip of your nose in the whipped cream on your birthday cake. So this process of bodily making letters that consist of one stroke is called writing. Please do not call it typography, just because it happens to use letters.

Lettering takes a step beyond writing. When doing lettering you always use drawn letters. These are letters whose significant parts are made of more than one stroke. The term 'drawn letters' reminds us again of pen and paper. The scope of lettering is of course much greater than the letterforms one can draw on paper. It also takes in large neon letters on buildings. Letters cut on gravestones are lettering too. It is impossible to cut the whole or the significant part of a letter with just one blow. But you can scratch a letter with one bodily movement, and then that has to be termed writing.

Another great difference between lettering and writing is the fact that in writing there is no possibility of correction. One of the

send you with separate post. The students'
works you see in it were done during the
same period, when the Bauhaus was in Des-
sau. But they are much better, more serious
than the Bauhaus works. Above all they are
more fundamental, the approach is <modern>
and timeless. There is an idea behind it's
curriculum. The man who was responsible

Not very encouraging news,
I am afraid; I spoke to Farm: whilst they
were very keen on the project before he
spoke to us about it, 'somebody' put the
lid on it' (as Farm said) + he is busily
trying to take it off again.
This means in reality long
delay (profuse apologies from HZ) and
he puts his chances of success at
this moment no higher than 20-25%.

*Two samples of writing. The first (3.3) is an experienced hand that produces
– without neglecting speed – a classical humanist italic. The second (3.4) is a
very common scribble: meant only for a short life and for one reader.*

essential characteristics of lettering is the much sought-after possibility to reconsider and correct. Lettering seems to have more in common with typography than writing does, because, in much lettering work, the letterforms look very much like printing types. But this is a false connection. Lettering does indeed stand between writing and typography, but only because of the fact that you can move its letters around after they have been made. For example, lettering is all that you can do with rub-down letters, however 'typographic' they may look. Rub down the word 'typography' from a sheet of Helvetica letters and this still has nothing to do with typography. Neither does it have anything to do with writing: the letters are drawn and not written. Letters rubbed down to make words may, in skilful hands, look typographic; but the spacing and alignment are determined by hand, and this defines the process as lettering.

In typography, the composition of the word, as well as the making of the letters, is regulated by machine-fabrication. This is so even in the simplest case, of composing metal type by hand. The bodies of the type and the spaces ensure this dimension of machine-fabrication; as does the setting-stick, which works as an elementary machine. The system extends beyond the word: to the line, to the whole column or page of text. The size and position of appearing elements (i.e. visible when printed) can be exactly specified. This is done with a measuring system that is particular to that machine, or with a more generally used system. As the word 'specified' indicates, this information can be given to someone else to carry out, and the process can be repeated exactly on another occasion. These two things are natural to typography, but are essentially impossible in writing and lettering.

Writing, lettering, and typography have in fact very little in common with each other, except that all three processes use the signs that we call letters. Each process gives a certain visual character to its output. And the outputs of all three processes are constrained by the limits of the human perceptual system. Of course, writing and lettering are also limited by the manual skills of the writer or letterer.

These three categories may not be absolutely separate from each other. The more experience you have, the more exceptions to the distinctions you will find. And a further fundamental distinction between typographic and other characters will be made in the next chapter. So an absolute or theological definition is not the point. But the definitions are meant as working guidelines, as a way of understanding essentials.

Each of these mediums has its own circumstance and character, its own scope and limits, its own freedoms, its own history. All of these things should be understood and cared for. I think the three mediums should not be mixed: at least not in ignorance.

A new printing type

Two samples of lettering. One (3.5) by W. A. Dwiggins, uses all the possibilities of reconsideration and correction that lettering offers. The result is some very 'typographic' looking words. The other (3.6) by Imre Reiner is pure lettering, not trying to be anything else.

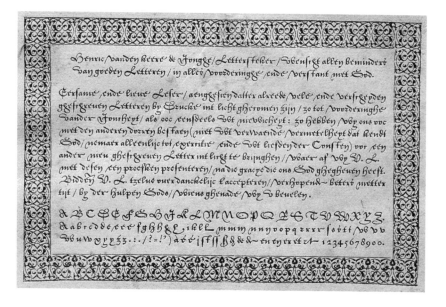

Two samples of typography. The first (3.7) is a civilité type cut by Hendrik
van den Keere: an imitation of a polite handwriting style of its time (c. 1570).
The second (3.8), Jonathan Hoefler's Egiziano Filigree, clearly wants to imitate
commercial hand-lettering of the nineteenth century. But both are fully typographic letters: text set in them can be repeated exactly, provided the right speci-
fication is given. This, and only this, distinguishes typography from writing and
lettering. For a translation of Van den Keere's text, see p. 188.

4 Type: a game of black and white

As the last chapter has shown, only some letters are typographic letters. Nowadays type may look like almost anything. There are no rules. You cannot recognize type by its form, use, or treatment. But it distinguishes itself from other kinds of letters – and this has always been true – by being intended for reproduction and by the way in which it is designed to form words. This way of making words is like a process of prefabrication. Typographic letters are words made and reproduced by means of machinery, whether digital or any other kind. A manual typewriter is perhaps the simplest form of typographic machine. This is now the only possible definition of type; but maybe it was always the only possible definition. Some readers may find this too simple. But I do not know of a better definition of type that covers present developments and those of the past too.

What makes a letter a letter, and a word a word? It is an old story, which one cannot avoid retelling. It all depends on an awareness of and a respect for the shapes between and within the letters. The white shapes make the background, the black shapes make the foreground. The background makes the foreground, and the other way around. Change one, and you change the other too [4.1]. It really is a game of black and white.

You learn to play this game first by learning to look at the spaces within the characters: the counters. They have to be equal in optical value [4.2, 4.3]. For example, the counter of n has to be equivalent to that of m. Characters don't mean very much on their own, so we put them together to make words. In doing this we have to deal with another problem: namely the spaces between the letters. These spaces have to be in balance with each other and, at the same time, in balance with the spaces within the characters [4.4]. Do this and you can create an acceptable word-image.

We are dealing here with a fundamental principle of design: the creation, testing and, if necessary, readjustment of order. In graphic

4.1
You cannot change the foreground without changing the background.
It is a unity.

and typographic design this order starts with the word-image. Every
student graphic designer needs to be aware of this, certainly when
working with present-day software. Writing with a broad nib is an essential foundation: not because of some vague notion of tradition or
sense of monkish duty, but because there is no more direct way for a
student to grasp this basic principle of design. Writing with a broad-
nib pen helps students develop a consciousness of two-dimensional
space and visual rhythm that is independent of time, style, and
technique.

The basic principle of creating order in foreground and background goes for all visual messages, no matter what technique is
used. The more formal the character of the design, the more this
principle holds true. If visual form and content are very informal this
role might become less applicable. Take two banal examples. A sign
system for an airport has to be very legible, and so it has to be very
formal in character. But my shopping list might as well be a barely
legible piece of scribbling; despite the fact that I am a type designer.

The less you observe this principle of balance, the less legible
will the result be, no matter when or how it was done [4.5]. Ignorance
of this means that many messages look formal without being very
readable: awkward both to look at and to read. Nobody complains,
because, at first sight, it looks plausible. But in fact we are looking
here at something like my shopping list, only scribbled with formal
means. The creators of this message seem to think that quality is

4.2

In A *we see a distorted word-image. The counter of the n is too small. If we want to improve it, the result would be as in* B. *Looking again at* A, *it is also possible to regard the counters of the m as too wide in comparison with those of the n. Then we would make the m narrower, and* C *could be the result.*

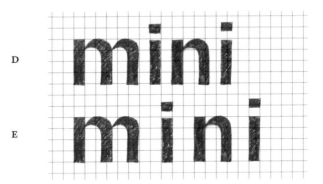

4.3

D *and* E *show another problem. Both make use of the same characters, yet their word length differs a great deal. The space between the letters in* D *is narrow but acceptable compared with the counters. In* E *the spaces between the letters are more or less equal with the counters.* D *looks good when used in this size, while* E *works best in small sizes.*

minimum

Johann Herder first proclaimed in 1772 that the basis of a nation was a language with its oral, traditional songs and stories. If there is a language, then it must be written down, given an alphabet and

minimum

standardized by deliberate selection from all its local variants. A dictionary must be written, and grammar must be provided for the children. A history of the people must be compiled. Folk-tales

minimum

and poetry must be collected and published to lay the base for a modern culture – or for a 'national intelligentsia' which will go on to compose a national literature.

4.4

At the top: a very restless gathering of words. The spaces within characters (the counters), and between them, differ constantly. The thickness of strokes is irregular too. The second text looks better at first sight. Now the counters are harmonized and there are no longer any striking differences of weight. But space between characters is not balanced, and so reading the text is still a tough assignment. In the third example, space between characters has been improved: the text is easy for the eye to scan, and thus easy to read. If we want to make text legible, certain basic visual and perceptual facts have to be observed. But if we want to irritate people, we know exactly what to do.

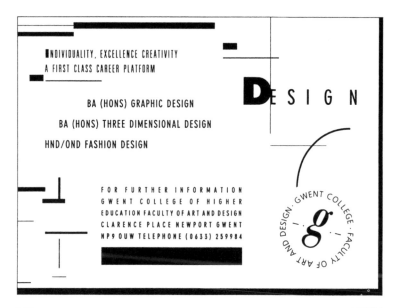

4.5

These signs carry comparable messages. One is produced with computers.
In the other just pens and scissors are used. One does its job badly (spot the post-
code!); the other very well. Visual effect does not depend on technology.

28

based on means of production. So a pencil-written message is always lesser than a piece of real typesetting. It is not true. Quality in visual messages is in the first place a matter of proper configuration, and not the result of a certain technique of production.

At the root of configuration or overall visual arrangement is the design of the word. This element of design used to be beyond the reach of most people and was also more fixed materially than it is now. Knowledge – or ignorance – of how to treat words has not changed much over the years. Misuse of type has nothing directly to do with computers and DTP-software. But now anyone can easily change the quality of the word-image. Anyone who, no matter how, gives language a visual form, with pre-existing letters that they call up themselves, is creating words. By using all the possibilities of determining the space between letters and between words this user will change the word-image. And this, in the end, is also true of someone who designs a typeface. Though it might seem that the type designer's aim is to make new characters, the real goal is to create a new word-image with a quality that differs from what is already available.

A word-image can have many different qualities. Here one can point out the difference between designing typographic characters and the same process for other kinds of letters. Take, for example, a logotype, or words on packaging, or an inscription cut in stone. When we are making characters that are not type, the content of the message that has to be given form is already known. Here one is giving form to given words and so making word-images that will never vary. This makes it 'easy'. You can focus just on this word-image. Someone designing a typeface does not have this given information. Their task is to ensure that the result looks good no matter what language or what words are set in these characters. (And, to keep things simple, this leaves the size of letters out of the discussion.) To be more specific, the word-image has to reach a good or at least an acceptable level of quality, no matter what character combinations occur. We can put this fundamental difference between typographic and other characters alongside the distinctions made in chapter 3.

4.6

Two counters that are different in shape but yet have more or less the same value: their surface area is about 200 mm².

To solve this problem of typeface design, we come back to the golden rule: space between characters has the same optical value to space within characters. You soon discover that this space is also a certain surface area. The troublesome thing is that this quantity of space has to fit into different shape [4.6]. These shapes are usually of a kind that make the surface area hard to measure. In short, a type designer is someone who is always measuring the areas of constantly varying shapes. When a shape has an area that is too great or too small, this shape will disturb the word-image. Experienced type designers develop a keen eye for this. They search constantly for imperfections and make corrections.

The space within a character can be divided into subcategories. There is the closed space or 'counter', strictly defined: as in 'o' or 'p'. The second kind is the almost closed counter: as in 'n' or 'a'. Third is the open counter: as in 'c' or 'z'. It is not so difficult to put characters next to each other properly when they contain closed or nearly closed counters [4.7, 4.8]. And when these shapes are very simple and easily perceived – then of course it is simple and easy. But things get harder when characters with open counters have to be fitted in. The golden rule breaks down here, and has to be modified.

If we insert a character with an open counter, we soon discover that there is no clear border between the space that belongs to the inner area of the character and the space that belongs to the area

4.7

The area between the two n's differs in shape from the area within each letter, but again its surface area is about 200 mm².

4.8

Put an o next to an n. Somewhere in the two dark areas around the x-height and the baseline there lies the border that marks off the area between the letters from the space above and below the word. Exactly where we draw the border is a matter of personal judgment. Such areas of doubt make the idea of perfect spacing an impossibility.

4.9

Put a z next to an a and you have a further problem. Where does the z start? The hatched space is an example of a double-function area. This area belongs to the inside as well as to the outside of the z. It is clear of course that the serif makes this area smaller and more defined.

between the two characters. This makes them difficult to measure. The way to resolve this is to understand that a certain part of the adjoining space has a double function. This area is inner-space and outer-space at the same time [4.9]. This doubly functioning area stands on the border. It is not fixed, but moves and differs in size when the characters are enlarged or reduced. Another problem is the fact that everyone will define this area a bit differently. So it is certainly not objectively exact or constant.

These areas of double function (and of doubt) are everywhere in the word-image – in text. The importance of serifs now becomes clear. Serifs help the designer and – I strongly suspect – the reader to define inner- and outer-space more definitely and more easily. And precisely because of these areas, a perfectly balanced typeface does not and cannot exist. Any attempt to make such a typeface would be a waste of time. Even if this was possible, perfectly balanced characters are visually without interest. This is not the issue, even within professional type design. The issue is to develop and find good balance based on and using these doubtful imperfections.

This, when it comes down to it, is all the knowledge you need to make word-images. And this knowledge runs as an invisible thread – in fact very visible – through all typographic history. It is a history that consists largely of the quest for balance, and of how to reinvent and redefine balance.

5 Comparing typefaces

Comparing typefaces is difficult, especially for students. 'Why is the a
of this typeface better than the a of another one?' The question hardly
makes sense: typefaces are sums of parts. And final judgement of a
typeface may indeed be impossible and not worth attempting. But
we can at least make clear what factors to look for when considering
a typeface.

One can divide typefaces into two main categories. There are
those that have a visual quality that draws attention to itself: in use,
they work as much like illustrations as like text that you read. Then
there are those typefaces that just work on the level of textual communication. There is no point in mixing these categories. There is no
use in comparing the headline typeface Mistral (designed by Roger
Excoffon) with the typeface Romanée (by Jan van Krimpen). What I
want to discuss is how to compare Romanée with Plantin.

Making comparisons between typefaces that have a strong illus-
trational quality may be harder than comparing typefaces designed
for textual communication. A comparison between Mistral and one
of Neville Brody's typefaces will be a very subjective matter [5.1].
One might only be able to say that Mistral has a fresh, lively, hand-
drawn quality that belongs to its time and place – France in the early
1950s – while Brody's Industria may remind one of what was most
fashionable in London in the 1980s. Having said that, there is not
much more to say – or, if so, it lies outside the scope of this book.

Now all of this may imply that typefaces made just as text carriers are removed from the question of personal taste. That is not true,
of course. But these typefaces do present us with a dimension that
can be discussed rationally and with some degree of objectivity. This
is because their proper use is bound by the limitations of the human
perceptual system.

We do not know exactly what a person – 'an average human
being' – can see comfortably: not even when they are reading. If type

Aa Bb Cc Dd Ee Ff Gg Hh
Ii Jj Kk Ll Mm Nn
Oo Pp Qq Rr Ss Tt Uu
Vv Ww Xx Yy Zz
1 2 3 4 5 6 7 8 9 0

Aa Bb Cc Dd Ee Ff Gg Hh Ii
Jj Kk Ll Mm Nn Oo Pp Qq Rr
Ss Tt Uu Vv Ww Xx Yy Zz
1 2 3 4 5 6 7 8 9 0

5.1
Typefaces that breathe the air of their times, and which can hardly be compared: Roger Excoffon's Mistral (France in the 1950s) and Neville Brody's Industria (London in the 1980s).

is too small, it demands too much attention from the reader, who has
constantly to decipher the characters. With all this energy devoted
to simply seeing, there is not much left over for understanding the
content of the text. Type can also be too narrow or too wide. These
dimensions are all defined, in the last analysis, by the counter. Counters that are too narrow do not give enough time (fractions of a second)
for readers to work out what they have seen. We may get the feeling
that we are looking not at letters but at some bar codes. Type that
is too wide gives us too much time, and we forget what we have just
been reading. Then we have to spell it all out, to get the message.
There is some mean or average value that defines the ratio of height to
width in the counters of roman type. Of course in display typography
the extremes of this ratio can be far apart. But with type for continuous text and serious reading, the ratio of height to width in counters
cannot vary so much. This ratio then becomes a battleground constantly fought over by type designers. They tend to look for the most
efficient counter: as tall and as narrow as possible. This may result in
a typeface that occupies the least space over a whole page, while re-
maining entirely readable.

The quest for this perfect counter is, I think, rather a useless one.
It has already been found many times over. In fact it has been found
every time someone has looked for it. This is certainly the case if the
designer has tried to work for the average reader. There are a huge
number of average human beings: each one will be different from the
other, with a different kind of eyesight and different habits of perception. The limits on a design only become clear when you are designing
for a very specific kind of reader (with impaired vision, for example)
or specific circumstances of production or use (low-grade printing, in-
struction manuals). But otherwise, you are dealing not with the limits
of a design, but with the limits created by the perceptual capacities
of millions of people at a reading distance of 40 centimetres.

Text typefaces are often compared by showing a small sample of
each at the same size: 12 point Plantin and 12 point Romanée, say [5.2].
But this does not tell us much. For one thing, and as is well known, the

Plantin word▌space
32 pt Plantin

Romanée word▌space
32 pt Romanée

Johann Herder first proclaimed in 1772 that the basis
of a nation was a language with its oral, traditional
songs and stories. If there is a language, then it must

12 / 16 Plantin

Johann Herder first proclaimed in 1772 that the basis of a nation
was a language with its oral, traditional songs and stories. If there
is a language, then it must be written down, given an alphabet and

12 / 16 Romanée

5.2

*Comparing typefaces by their nominal size tells us nothing; it reveals
merely differences in design proportion. No conclusions can be drawn from
this, except that typefaces (even conventional ones) differ from each other.*

Plantin x x Romanée
32 pt Plantin & 38 pt Romanée

Johann Herder first proclaimed in 1772 that the basis
of a nation was a language with its oral, traditional
songs and stories. If there is a language, then it must

12 / 16 Plantin

Johann Herder first proclaimed in 1772 that the basis of
a nation was a language with its oral, traditional songs
and stories. If there is a language, then it must be written

13.8 / 16 Romanée

5.3

*This is what is needed: with equal x-heights, you can compare typefaces.
Starting with 12 pt Plantin, you find that Romanée has to be 13.8 pt nominal
size, to achieve equal x-height. Comparing the same text set in these sizes,
you see that Romanée is the more efficient of the two.*

Johann Herder first proclaimed in 1772 that the basis of
a nation was a language with its oral, traditional songs
and stories. If there is a language, then it must be written
down, given an alphabet and standardized by deliberate

12 / 16 Plantin

Johann Herder first proclaimed in 1772 that the basis of
a nation was a language with its oral, traditional songs
and stories. If there is a language, then it must be written
down, given an alphabet and standardized by deliberate

13.8 / 16 Romanée

5.4
*Another factor that effects good and efficient setting of text is word-space.
5.2 and 5.3 both use 100% word-spaces. In Plantin this is much too large;
in Romanée it is acceptable. In the Plantin text above, the word-space is
changed to 80%.*

Johann Herder first proclaimed in 1772 that the basis of
a nation was a language with its oral, traditional songs
and stories. If there is a language, then it must be written
down, given an alphabet and standardized by deliberate

12 / 15 Plantin

Johann Herder first proclaimed in 1772 that the basis of
a nation was a language with its oral, traditional songs
and stories. If there is a language, then it must be written
down, given an alphabet and standardized by deliberate

13.8 / 16 Romanée

5.5
*Line increment is another vital factor in setting text. Plantin can do with
a smaller line increment; in the text above it is reduced to 15 pt. This increases
the number of lines on a page, and thus improves efficiency. To investigate
efficiency fully, you have to look at layout: another book.*

nominal size of a typeface is not an exact description of its appearing size. You can make the capital heights of the samples the same, but even this does not really help. The real issue in these typefaces is their visual impact, their strength, and their comfort at reading sizes. It is this that you want to compare. If you make the capitals equal in height, then you can compare capitals. But capitals are not so important in reading.

The impression one has of a page of text is largely determined by what happens within the x-height of the characters, and, of course, also by all the variables that a designer or compositor can determine (letter-space, word-space, line increment, etc). If you standardize and so discount those variables, then you are left with what we might call x-height performance. It is this that gives a typeface its quality and value. So then, to make a true comparison between typefaces, one has to make x-heights equal [5.3]. Then you can judge on level ground. This should be done at reading sizes. You cannot do it larger and make a transfer in your mind to how it might be at reading size.

To make the test, first print out sample passages of text in the typefaces at equal x-height. Do it at high resolution: on an image setter not a laser printer. Now look. Does one typeface look blacker than the other? How is this blackness achieved? Are the thin parts strong enough? Or are they too thin, and visually irritating? Can the overall effect of this text match accompanying illustrations? These are the first and must important things to look for. Then you can go on to compare the effects of ascenders and descenders, simply by setting the same text to the same length of line and with the same line increment. You can also tell something about efficiency in this way. By 'efficiency', I mean not merely the number of characters that fit in a line of a certain length. But also, how large should the word-space be? They may be adjusted [5.4]. The vertical dimension of text-setting is part of this too. How much space between lines is needed for satisfactory reading? At a given size, some typefaces need a greater line increment than others [5.5]. And, of course, all these factors interact with each other. Such a test is the only reasonable way to answer the questions: which typeface looks best? and which is the most efficient?

Evaluation does not stop here. There are other dimensions of quality. One important area of consideration is completeness of the character set. Does the typeface have non-lining figures, a bold italic, small capitals, italic small capitals, sufficient ligatures, sufficient kerning pairs …? Then you might ask if it is satisfactory when used in large sizes. Is it equipped with a suitable display version? Does this please you at 36 point? Is it too weak? Or too strong and stiff? And here we are back in the field of personal taste.

Punchcutting in its contexts

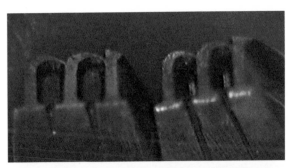

A clear difference of opinion between Claude Garamond (top left) and
Hendrik van den Keere (top right). Both punches belong to the same set,
originally made by Claude Garamond, which was then modified by
Van den Keere. To gain 'efficiency', ascenders and descenders were made
shorter: as in the picture of the two p's (here Hendrik is on the left, Claude
on the right). But Van den Keere could not resist adding a lowercase m too.
It wasn't really necessary for the job, because what was being modified was
the space above and below the x-height, and thus line increment. Notice
too the remarkable difference in depth of the counters.

6 Letters and the Italian intellect

The first typographic letters seemed to be very formal written letters. This is logical: it could hardly have happened any other way. Gutenberg could never have thought of making letters other than those that looked like formal written letters. His ideal would have been to make type indistinguishable from formal writing. So the goal of typography at first had nothing to do with type or design: it had everything to do with saving time. Producing multiple copies of books faster than they could be written was the point of typography: no more and no less.

Type came to be seen as separate from writing only after about 1500, and this happened mainly in Italy. Although the Italian humanists of that time still saw type as intimately bound up with writing, it is in their work that we can first see the idea of type. And this 'idea' we can call 'design': a strong consciousness of the forms of letters and their disposition on a page. Humanism in Italy made itself felt before the 1460s, when the first printing presses were established there. But its peak, which we call the Renaissance, coincided with this first flourish of Italian typography.

The influence of these intellectuals on typography was actually very strong. The humanists were the users of print and they defined the premises and assumptions behind typography. These premises were however not much more than an intellectual fashion based on some mistakes. The principal, notorious mistake concerned the minuscule letters ('lowercase' or small letters) which they saw used in classical literature, and which they took as a model and copied. They assumed that this hand was the writing of classical antiquity: but in fact these texts were medieval copies, written in what we call the Carolingian minuscule.

The fashion of the Italian Renaissance entailed an exaggerated desire to emulate and imitate what was imagined to be classical antiquity. The Italian humanists did not take tradition as given, but made up their own variations on it. They certainly respected the culture of

Aldus Manutius Romanus Antonio Codro Vrceo.S.P.D.

Collegimus nuper Codre doctissime quotquot habere potuimus græcas epistolas, eásque typis nostris excusas, duobus libris publicamus, præter multas illas Basilii. Gregorii, & Libanii, qûas cû primum fuerit facultas, imprimendas domi seruamus. Auctores uero, quo rum epistolas damus, sunt numero circiter quíq; & tri ginta, ut in ipsis libris licet uidere. has ad te, qui & latinas & græcas litteras in celeberrimo Bononiési gymnasio publice profiteris, muneri mittimus, tum ut à te discipulis ostédantur tuis, quo ad cultiores litteras capesfendas incendantur magis, tum ut apud te sint Aldi tui μνημόσυνον & pignus amoris.   Vale Venetiis quinto decimo calendas maias M.ID.

6.1

A colophon from one of Aldus Manutius's books. The type, cut by the Italian punchcutter Francesco Griffo, is one the most important humanist romans – and the model for Monotype Bembo. (Epistolea, Venice, 1499.)

6.2

The minuscule (left) was adopted by the humanists and they 'improved' it: made it look lighter and gave it a double serif translating it into printing type (right). But can anyone really write these letters? They don't appear in any of the famous writing books.

classical antiquity, but considered themselves superior to it. The humanists started to improve on antiquity in everything: architecture, sculpture, painting, writing, and they improved on its letterforms as well. Imagined superiority has to have somewhere to manifest itself. These improvements are really artificial additions, rather than developments occurring as part of a long evolving tradition. In fact the main changes within type occur over a period of about fifty years.

Now take this sample of printing [6.1]. Even without knowing the title of the book from which it comes, we know that this must be a humanist text. Why? Because it uses the new letters. Or more exactly: the letters that these modern humanists imagined were a real product of classical Roman antiquity, but then improved to become better than the work of those ancients.

The humanist letters present us with a puzzle: a double serif pasted onto the minuscule [6.2]. If we want to solve this mystery we have to go on examining and worrying about what happened in Italy in the years between 1460 and 1500. Harry Carter put it like this: 'The humanists' copying hand used for the classics had reached a very high polish by the time that printing was introduced to Italy, and scholars and architects were much concerned with collecting epigraphs from ancient Roman monuments and *thinking out rules* for reproducing the lettering.' And, quoting from one of the protagonists: 'Erasmus had a decided and declared preference for Roman letters, as might be expected. He praised "a handwriting that is elegant, clear, and distinct, representing *Latin words by Latin elements*".'* This tells us gently something about the climate of humanist opinion on letters. I could put it more crudely. The Italian humanists were modernists interested in the new. They wanted something different. They felt they were better than ever before in every department of culture. So their scribes – essential people who wrote down and made the new culture manifest – began (rather suddenly) to abandon old, heavy scripts, and to make a new one that breathed the new mentality. Since the human-

---

* Carter, *A view of early typography*, pp. 70, 78; the italics are mine.

6.3

*An ordinary minuscule written in Italy in the fifteenth century. The scribe
just wrote it, without too much effort. Nowadays this looks rather messy,
but it is still very legible. This quality of writing was common practice before
the invention of typography.*

6.4

*Writing by Nicolas Jarry in France, from 1651, makes a clear contrast with
6.3. A page like this could not have been 'written' without the model of
printed pages.*

ists considered themselves to be part of a larger movement – perhaps they were the first real world citizens – national boundaries, cultural peculiarities and differences were no hindrance for them. This made it easy for the new letters to travel all over Europe, finding acceptance everywhere, and resulting in our world now, in which we seem to have unconditional admiration for what we call the Italian Renaissance.

Looking at the humanist manuscripts, they do look typograph-ic. We wonder which came first, these letters or the printed ones? Even just the space between the lines, or the line increment, seems familiar to us. It is what we do with lines of type. So we admire these beautiful pages of typeset-like writing, which reach their peak a hun-dred or so years later on [6.4], in the cases of museums or in the pic-tures of books about writing. This is a view from a distance.

These humanist letters are often made of bits and pieces glued together, with great pain. They balance on the border between writ-ing and drawing. In his desire to rationalize even the minuscule into geometric form, the scribe had to do battle with the natural or bodily conditions of writing.

The pure roman is a broken script, consisting mainly of straight pen strokes that stand at 90 degrees to the baseline. This stroke looks rather simple, but it is one of the most difficult strokes to make. To make it easier to execute this stroke, a scribe could do three things [6.5]. First: thicken up the stroke. And then: put strokes close to each other, using the previous one as a reference and guideline. Third: avoid the niggling question of straightness by reducing the straight middle

easy   *difficult*

6.5
Before typography, text was often written in rather fat 'wavy' hands, for practical and economic reasons.

6.6

This manuscript (from Ferrara, 1475) shows a strange mixture of elements: medieval guide-lines, humanist capitals, considerable space between the lines, a rather light overall colour in the text-block. Even the letters themselves present a mixture of gothic cursive with a light, open humanist minuscule. The ingredients are blended together smoothly. In theory such a mix should not exist. But one finds it often in manuscripts from that time.

part as much as possible. Then you end up with a rather bold, narrow script: a script that cannot be described as being built up out of Latin elements, as Erasmus had in mind. Certainly for writing bulky texts in reading sizes these 'tricks' are very practical and they were applied for centuries, until questioned by the humanist taste for light and openness.

Pure, formal written romans are rare if not unknown before 1500. By about that time it seems that typography forced the scribes to become more ordered and coherent. One can find common procedures. But if you look at manuscripts from between about 1450 and 1500, it seems that Italian formal writing was in confusion: each scribe had his own way of forming characters. For this research, you need to look further than the handful of specimens of humanist script that decorate our 'history of printing type' books.

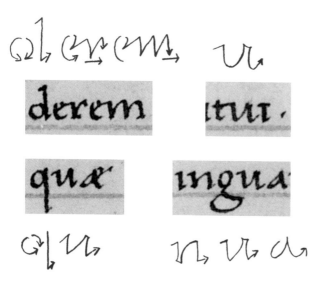

6.7

Details of the manuscript shown in 6.6. We can distinguish three approaches to the formation of letters: gothic cursive (m, n, u); italic (e, a); and humanist broken construction (d, q, g).

49

For example, look at this piece of writing [6.6]. It looks humanistic. And it is that, in part. But, looking closer, you see a mixture of different worlds. There are the typical Renaissance Roman capitals. The layout is humanist: rather light in colour, generous space between lines. The weight of the small letters is also on the light side. But the drawn guidelines for the text are a medieval practice; so too is the Lombardic capital D.

The small letters offer a nice riddle. Some characters are pure humanist minuscules: p, d, q, b, g. But if we look at h, n, m, u, and especially r, we see a true gothic cursive: the very opposite of the light and open humanist minuscule [6.7]. All these ingredients are mixed and made into a well-balanced unity. According to schematic history, this manuscript cannot exist. But in fact it is no exception. The world of writing had great freedom before 1500, and 'exceptions' to the humanist rule continued to be made after that date.

6.8

At first Italian humanists had to use what was available, such as this rotunda for texts by Giovanni Pico della Mirandola. The typical humanist minuscule took at least 30 years of experiment before the standard was set by Aldus Manutius. (Apologia, Naples, 1487.)

The humanist pages that we are most familiar with were written around 1500, by which time the typographic roman was well on its way in intellectual circles. Typography had then begun to prod the Italian scribes in their back: 'show me what you can do!' If it was true that 'typical humanist script' was very common in 1450, then we might believe the story that roman type evolved from humanist handwriting. But it didn't seem to happen quite like that. The typical humanist manuscript pages show up too late: by thirty years or so. It seems that scribes and printers influenced each other, and that the result is a cross-fertilization between the two worlds.

One has to assume that the humanist scribes, and the intellectual elite behind them, hardly knew how they wanted their letters to look. It took them quite a while to solve the problems of constructing their desired letters – supposing that these problems could ever be solved. So, by the time that their preferred or even their own texts were going into print, they had not been able to set a clear standard in letters, such as had been provided by textura and rotunda. They had to make do with what was available [6.8]. And the scribe's doubts and indecisions led to a gap between written letters and their typographic representation. Type design was born.

In the climate of Italian humanism it was possible to come up with strange, super-rational creations. Reason was followed at any cost. The Roman capital letters were accepted into writing and type without great changes. These letters were rationalized by the geometrical schemes of Felice Feliciano, Luca Pacioli, and the others we are familiar with [6.9]. Such schemes tell us more about humanism than they tell us about designing usable letters.

The capital serif can be explained by a baseline, a straight vertical stroke, and two circles [6.10]. How pure! The minuscule serif is too organic, too much part of the main stroke, to be so easily rationalized. Nevertheless this capital serif was preferred over the easier, more fitting minuscule serif, and pasted onto the minuscule stem. It was symmetrical and logical : logical and symmetrical was it!

This drawing-board or even armchair thinking gave the scribe

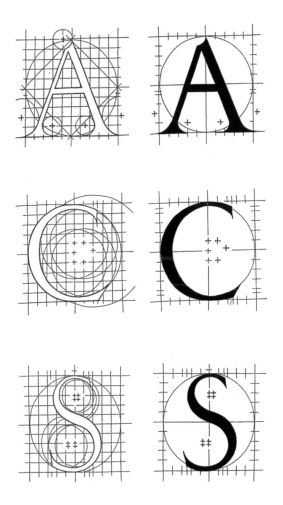

6.9

*A nice image with an air of confidence, made by Albrecht Dürer. However,
such diagrams do not really tell us much about capital letterforms in use.
The proportions given in these schemes could not be applied to printing type. The
real value of such drawings is in telling us something about humanist mentality:
the attempt to get a grip on form by describing it mathematically.*

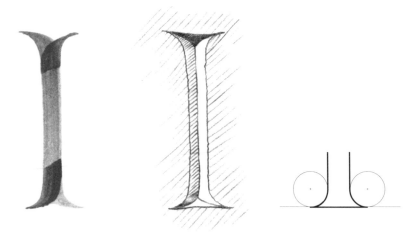

6.10

*The Roman capital: how it was written with a flat brush in Antiquity (left),
what the Romans did to preserve it in stone (middle), and how the humanists
of Renaissance Italy explained this form to themselves (right). In humanist
eyes, a symmetrical serif was mathematically 'truer', and thus superior to the
minuscule serif of 6.5.*

inmhulocdqe apbrsgfffftttt

6.11

*A highly rationalized twentieth-century hand (in this case, written by
Jan Tschichold). Such writing has acted as a kind of filter, through which
we view its humanist sources.*

big problems. The rational approach to the minuscule and the bodily conditions of implementing this approach were in conflict with each other. This must be the reason for the scribes not being able to set any formal standard that could be followed in typography.

But ways were found, because the intellectually beautiful result was more important than the making. We need to adjust our conception of the humanistic minuscule. We tend to imagine it as in illustration 6.11; but 6.12 shows (it is a little exaggerated) the ideal that some late fifteenth-century scribes were working towards. The reality lay between these two extremes. Meanwhile, printing was getting started, with the help of goldsmiths, some of whom began to specialize in making punches for type: the punchcutters. By contrast with the difficulties that the symmetrical serif gave to scribes, the punchcutters managed to make it easily enough. They just did it, like they could do anything in steel: portraits, buildings, landscapes ... So these newfangled letters were no more than another job for the punchcutter.

conclusione ego declarando dixi

6.12
Four centuries were needed before the humanist ideal could be realized in the German Weimar Republic. To make avant-garde modernist letters, all that the fifteenth-century scribes would have had to have done was take a really big quill – a tube with 'walls' 0.5 mm thick – and then to cut a point as wide as this thickness, so that the width was as great as its height: a 'broad nib' with a square point.

7 The place of the punch in type production

The first movable types were cast in lead (or an alloy of lead). The letterform – the typeface – that was finally printed on paper was defined by the punch. The men who cut the punches were the designers of typefaces; though 'design' in our modern sense of planning, and drawing-as-instruction, had not then begun. And, for reasons explained in this book, design in this sense could not happen in cutting punches by hand.

Punches stand near the start of the long process of making type and typefaces. The whole process is shown in the pictures reproduced in this chapter, which were drawn and engraved in France at the end of the seventeenth century as part of the project of description of the trades carried out by the Académie Royale des Sciences in Paris. Though they anticipated by fifty years – and evidently provided the models for – the well-known engravings of the great French *Encyclopédie*, these pictures were published in full only in 1991.*

In the original prints these views are just the upper parts of larger engravings. In the lower two thirds of the prints, the tools used in making type were laid out and itemized. The picture of the type mould is also of this kind [7.1]. It is taken from another plate in the series, given over to the mould and its parts. Our diagram [7.2] tries

* See the article by James Mosley, 'Illustrations of typefounding engraved for the *Descriptions des arts et métiers* of the Académie Royale des Sciences, Paris, 1694 to c. 1700', *Matrix*, no. 11, 1991, pp. 60–80. We are indebted to James Mosley for help in providing copies of the engravings (copyright of the St Bride Library, London) used here as the originals of our reproductions. The descriptions of processes follow his annotations closely. Interested readers are urged to see the original article for a much fuller description of these plates and of what they show. The engravings of the mould are taken from a plate in this series in the possession of The Newberry Library, Chicago.

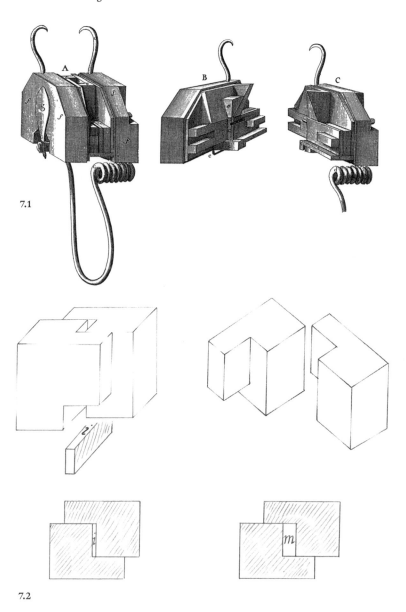

7.1

7.2

The mould: as seen in a plate from the series made for the Académie Royale des Sciences (7.1); and in drawings that show the principles of its operation (7.2).

56

to explain how it works: two parts that fit together, sliding to hold matrices of different widths.

The first picture in the set of five shows preparation of materials and making of counterpunches [7.3]. The two men (1, 2) at the forge are preparing a steel bar, to the size of a punch; a man (3) then cuts this bar to the required length; the punch is made square with a file (4). At the bench counterpunches are prepared: polished or faced on an oilstone (5), shaped with a file (6), tested for shape by making smoke-proofs from them (7). Finally (8), the counterpunch is struck into the blank that will become the punch.

In the second image [7.4], counterpunches or punches are shown being made. A blank is marked (1), worked on with a file or burin (2), cleared of loose metal by hammering it into lead (3), inspected after being smoke-proofed (4), and proofed again (5). Then the counterpunch or punch is heated on coals and (6) tempered by plunging it into cold water.

In the third picture matrices are made [7.5]. From right to left: trial pieces of type are smoke-proofed for justification (1); checked for alignment (2), set (3), and height to paper (4). The figure at the window (5) is dressing a matrix with a flat file. A trial cast is made (6). At the left (7), a punch is struck into a matrix blank.

The fourth in this series of views shows type being cast [7.6]. The two casters stand with ladles to either side of a furnace. The four other workmen are carrying moulds, in various stages of use.

In the last engraving, cast type is finished and ready for composition [7.7]. From left to right: type is held in a vice and 'jet' is broken off (1); it is rubbed on a stone (2); 'dressed' or shorn of rough parts (3); scraped with a knife (4); put into paper packets (5), one for each letter; or made up into founts (6) for customers who buy type that way.

Overleaf (7.3–7.7), the illustrations of typefounding from the set made for the Académie Royale des Sciences.

7.3   1   2   3   4   5   6   7   8

7.4   1   2   3 4 5   6

7.5   7   6 5   4   3 2   1

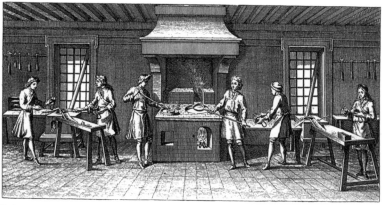

7.6

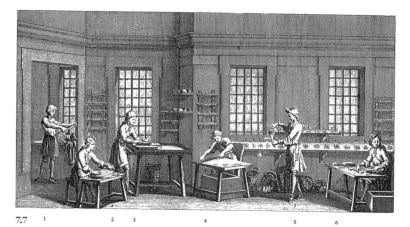

7.7   1   2   3   4   5   6

In summary, the whole process was as follows:
    a punch was cut
    a matrix was struck with the punch
    this matrix was justified and placed in a mould
    molten lead was poured into this mould
    the piece of type was taken out
    unnecessary material was removed from the type
    it was brought to a uniform height
    the type was set
    the type was inked and printed
    the image of the type (the typeface) could be seen on paper

8 The punchcutter and the historians

The people who made punches – the punchcutters – defined the final and visible forms of the typeface: forms that have been handed down to us and are often essentially unchanged today. Since the time when the typefaces we regard now as classical were first cut, the use of type has only increased. And now, with digitization, new devices and more producers, type has begun to be used more intensely and more widely still.

Punchcutting has never been sufficiently taken into account by the historians of typography. I suspect it has been seen too much as just a matter of manual dexterity. The notable exception here is the research done at the Plantin-Moretus Museum in the 1950s by Harry Carter, H. D. L. Vervliet, Matthew Carter, Mike Parker, and others. Their primary goal was to identify types and makers, and to restore punches. This research slowed down in the 1960s, as these people moved on to other things. But now, through their efforts, as well as through the work of the Museum's own staff, there is a place where, after making just a phone call for an appointment, you can handle this material and study it. We can be very grateful for this.

These researchers were often able to identify type; but, at least in what they wrote for publication, there is not much discussion of the process of making punches. Sometimes not just the letter-image but the punch as a whole – the way it was finished, and the physical character of the whole thing – can help considerably in identifying its maker or in determining whether it was a later addition to an already existing set. For example, Mike Parker was known to be able to identify the maker of a punch by looking at how it was finished. That is just one example of how an understanding of technique can help to fill in the missing pieces of a puzzle.

So the literature about the craft of punchcutting is very limited. For the most part, it consists of facts found in archives, discussion of these facts and debates with the previous writers on the subject. The result is that all the facts are put more exactly into chronological order. But the main questions – my main questions, at least – remain unanswered. What exactly is punchcutting for type? How did these men think about letterforms? What made them think that way? In short, what were or what could have been the designers' intentions? None of the historians answer these questions sufficiently. At most, there may be a paragraph or so: not much in comparison with the rest of the discussion. The punchcutter is constantly surrounded by foggy clouds of admiration. It is as if these writers are saying to us: 'Here are these facts, drink them in, and then take them for granted. But please don't ask for anything else, because we experts have no answers.'

The only works on punchcutting that have living value for us, as well as their purely historical importance, are the books by Fournier and by Moxon. These, together with some punches and matrices, are essentially all we have. (One could mention the information scattered in marginal notes and essays, by punchcutters or typefounders such as Fleischman, Breitkopf, Edward Prince, P. H. Rädisch.) Both Fournier and Moxon can be obtained with a little persistence in good editions. Both leave many questions unanswered. As already explained in chapter 1, the only thing I could do to find answers was to cut punches myself, to make the experience my own, and then work backwards to what lies behind the practice. So a main purpose of this book is to give a thorough explanation of punchcutting, its history, different traditions, its precision, and its effect on type design. Then the foggy clouds of admiration may be lifted.

9 Where does the punchcutter come from?

No letterpress, no punchcutter. That seems very obvious and logical. Punchcutting is now usually connected with typography and printing, so it could seem that the punchcutter came into existence with the invention of printing. But this is not true, for punchcutting is much older than printing and typography.

The invention of printing is not much more than the implementation of already available knowledge. This knowledge was taken out of its usual contexts, brought together, and put into another context. Then something else could be done with it, namely printing. Thus, in 1450, the principle of the press was familiar in other areas of manufacture. To print from a raised surface was also already being done. And punchcutting existed too. People impressed punches into wax to make seals. Makers of weapons and of everyday tools marked their products with them. Punches were used in the metal trade to mark a name on a product. And one very important organization used punches as the basis of its work: the mint [9.1]. Punches were even being printed onto paper.

To think of every letter as a separate thing, to make punches of each letter, to strike them into matrices, to make castings of a standard height and to make them rectangular so that they could easily be put side-by-side to compose words and then a line of text, and so that finally the lines head-to-foot could compose columns of text: this thought is 'the invention of printing and of typography'. It was a kind of elevated game of children's bricks. To make it possible, Gutenberg needed a mould that could easily be put together and also taken apart – to remove the cast letter. Further, it had to be easily adjustable in width. This mould is a valuable invention, and quite commonly regarded as the thing that was really invented in the invention of printing. But it is of secondary importance. The crucial new thing was the concept that led to the adjustable mould.

We know that the shadowy Gutenberg was a goldsmith, or at

9.1

*A coin from c. 1700. In the E the same fault can be seen repeated four times:
the lower arm of the letter is too thin and also it is broken. R is broken too, and O
is too bold. The faults in these letters and their exact repetition suggests something
about the die from which the coin was cast: that it was not engraved, but rather
made by hitting punches into it, probably by the method described by Benvenuto
Cellini. Enlarged from a real size of c. 20 mm diameter.*

least connected to the guild of goldsmiths, and he and his colleagues would have been very familiar with punchcutting. It was their work to make things such as punches for the mint and for seal-rings. These punches often had heraldic illustrations, and letterforms were incorporated too. One can compare them to the logotypes of present-day graphic design. The making of a punch was usually just a little piece of work that was a part of a larger piece of work. At least, it was like that if we believe Benvenuto Cellini (in an important early text on the subject, written around 1560). For every new coin, he made a number of punches for the lettering:

'... my custom was to cut out the heads, hands and feet of my figures on small steel punches, and thinking the work came clearer and got a better result, I struck these punches with dextrous strokes upon the seal with a hammer into their different places. Also you should make in a similar manner an alphabet of steel punches, likewise many other conceits according as taste prompts. When I was in Rome, or elsewhere, working in this line, I ofttimes amused myself by making new alphabets, each for its occasion, for they wear out soon, and I got much credit by my inventiveness. Your letters should be well formed, & shaped as a broadly cut pen might shape them; the strokes going up or down with the action of the hand, the letters being neither too fat and stumpy, nor too long and thin, for both these are unpleasing to behold, the moderately slim ones are the nicest to look at.'*

These letters were struck into the die by means of the smaller letter-punches. The die was in two pieces, one for each side. This was the punchcutter's real product. The coins were hit or pressed with it. For Benvenuto and his colleagues, it did not matter very much whether they had to cut lettering, a crown, or a portrait of an ancient ruler. In practice they often had to do all these things for one job.

In this light, it is more than likely that the first punchcutters would have been goldsmiths who also made punches for a printer.

* Cellini, *Treatises on goldsmithing and sculpture*, p. 65.

9.2

A set of currently available commercial letter-punches, for use in naming and numbering such things as machine parts or bicycle frames. They can be bought in good hardware shops.

Somebody wanted to start a printing business and needed type. So this aspiring printer would have gone to a friendly goldsmith, showed him a manuscript or a book from a competing printer, and said: 'Well, something like this. How much will it cost? How long will it take?' It sounds simple, but the process must have been like this in outline.

So the very first punchcutters, in the fifteenth century, were people who made punches on request. In other words, for them it was just a temporary job on the side. Things became interesting when printers themselves started to cut punches, and when goldsmiths or intending printers ended up as specialist punchcutters instead. By the time that Christopher Plantin was working in Antwerp, from the 1550s onwards, this activity of punchcutting had become a separate profession, although a very small and select one, about which it is hard to generalize. In Harry Carter's words: 'Printers financed and organized the making of type, but they took no other part in it. The tasks of cutting punches, striking and justifying matrices, mould-making, and casting were separate from printing and done by independent contractors. They needed great skill and experience and could only be done economically after a long specialized training.'* Later, in

---

* Carter, *A view of early typography*, p. 10.

the seventeenth century, the independent type foundry would come into existence, and punchcutters would tend to work for one of these firms. But for a time, in the sixteenth century, the cutting of new typefaces was in the hands of a number of independent workmen. It is hard to give any numbers based on research, but a wild guess might suggest that about 600 of them would have been required to supply all the punches needed to make type in the first hundred years of printing.

10 The rise and fall of the punchcutter

This book devotes much attention to the sixteenth century, and in particular to the years 1520–1600. This is an important period in the history of type, for several reasons. As discussed in chapter 6, the choice of capitals, minuscule, and italic was made for artificial and theoretical reasons, defined in large part by the Italian humanists. It was, however, the French and Flemish punchcutters who gave these letters their final shapes – who really consolidated their forms. They also succeeded in making a better marriage between the capital, minuscule, and italic. Further, a considerable part of all the punches and matrices that still survive derives from this period. So there is evidence, and the possibility of proving certain facts. Besides, during this time the punchcutter grew into someone more connected with the world of printing than the person still with one foot in the world of goldsmithing, as had been the case before 1500. Punchcutters from this period were themselves often editor-printer-publisher too, and so it is natural that they should have made the typographic material they needed themselves, rather than constantly having to fulfil the needs and wishes of somebody else. Often – it could hardly have been otherwise – these people were active in cultural-political and religious life. In fact, it is hard to imagine a tighter circuit between makers of typographic material, printers and the commercial world, and what was going on in the culture as a whole. As an example, I shall give an account of someone whose name hardly appears in the popular literature of typography.

One of the best punchcutters of this period, to be ranked with Garamond or Granjon, is Pierre Haultin. He was a punchcutter-printer-publisher as well as a Protestant. So in France at that time, he lived under the pressures of belonging to a forbidden sect. And I could add that he showed the more direct, down-to-earth mentality which distinguishes Protestants from their Roman Catholic colleagues. Looking behind Haultin's type, we might find him thinking along these lines:

'What use are these large and heavy bibles? I must be able to pick up my things and move quickly. What I need is a small pocket-bible which I can pack away in an instant. For this I need a very small and efficient roman. How small can I go?' So Haultin looked to the acceptable limit of size, and he found it at around 6 point. He was the first to cut a roman so small; and soon afterwards some italic and Greek. Smaller than this was not possible, for the simple fact that roman is not fit to use smaller than 6 point [10.1]. Haultin – I can assure you – was able to cut a roman even smaller than 6 point. But he did not do this: only because letters as small as that are no longer sufficiently readable.

Haultin proved here that he regarded type as absolutely different from writing. The influence of the written letter on size was being abandoned. No formal minuscules comparable to 6 point were written by the humanists. There are no manuscripts – or perhaps just a very few – with a line increment even near to 8 points. There were dextrous calligraphers who could write a minuscule comparable to 8 point in x-height. But often these letters are very bold and have long

10.1

*Probably the first 6 pt roman ever made was a type cut by Pierre Haultin: his Nonpareille Romaine. It was used frequently by Plantin from 1557. (*Libri regum ..., *Antwerp: Plantin, 1557.) See also 20.1.*

ANTIDOTARII. **2r**

flauo : quod cū difficilè reperiatur fupradiĉto vten-
dum eſt.

PAPAVERIS apud Dioſcoridem ſex ſunt
genera.Primum ſylueſtre rhęas diĉtum omnibus no
tum.Alterum,candidum,capitibus oblongis,ꞇcandi-
dis,ſemine albo: hoc etiam notum.Tertiū & Quar-
tum,nigrum,è quibus colligitur opium : ſemine ni-
gro ; vtrumque Dioſcoride papauer ſylueſtre etiam
dicitur: & illud notum eſt . Quintum papauer cor-
niculatum,ſic diĉtum,quod caput non proferat,ſed
ſiliquam oblongam & rotundam in corniculi modum,florem luteum,vulgo notum. Sextum papauer
ſpumeum vocatur,hoc incognitum eſt.Quoties pa-
paueris ſimpliciter & ſine adieĉtione mentio fit,ſem
per domeſticum,hoc eſt album intelligendum eſt.

Piper arbuſcule in India naſcētis fruĉtus eſt: quæ
inter initia vt ait Dioſc. prælongum fruĉtum veluti
ſiliquam,quod piper longum vocamus,profert ; ha-
bet intus aliquid tenui milio ſimile, quod dehiſcen-
tibus ſiliquis racemorum in modum prodit. Eorum
grana acerba candidum piper vocantur: matura verò,piper nigrum . Qui verò in Indiam nauigarunt,
piperiſque plantam viderunt, piper in planta bryo-
niæ ſimili naſci aſſerunt , diuerſiſque ex plantis longum & rotundum colligi.Nihil tamen intereſt. Nigrum eligi debet recens,grauiſsimum,plenum. Can
didum præfertur,non rugoſum,candidum,& graue,
Longum optimum, quod , dum frangitur , ſolidum
intus conſpicitur & compaĉtum,guſtu acerrimo lin
guamǫ mordens. Adulteratur longum herba ſimili:
ſed fucus depręhéditur,ſi in aquam immittatur; nam
adulterinū liqueſcit,legitimum verò ſolidū manet.

Pix è lignis pinguibus & reſinoſis fluit, præſertim
è pino. Quibuſdam tamen in locis,propter pini pe-
nuriam,ex picea,cedro,terebintho,cæteriſque ſimi-
libus cōgregatur eo quem infrà dicemus modo. Pix
C ſ naualiꞅ

10.2

A rather open but very efficient roman cut by Pierre Haultin.
*(*Antidotarium ... Carolus Clusius, *Antwerp: Plantin, 1561.)*

ascenders and descenders: so that, in the end, line increment is much
more than 8 points. It may not be impossible to write smaller than
8 point, but it is certainly awkward and tiring, whether or not the
manuscript is a formal one. Roman letters are absolutely unfit for
writing in a small x-height. Civilité and other letters much better suited to a small x-height, and to the human motor system, had already
been developed.

Haultin started to set his own standards. Now mentally apart
from goldsmithing and working within the world of printing, he was
fully aware of what was needed. He understood the possibilities that
steel provides, compared to the nib of a quill pen (the capacities of
which should not be underestimated either). Haultin is proof of the
punchcutter's consciousness: a mature craftsman who starts to explore and define the possibilities of his profession. He questions the
type size that it is possible for a human to manufacture, and instead
refers to what we can read. The dialogue of type with human perceptual capacities had begun.

Many changes and developments occurred in the years 1520–
1600. Music type was cut; the habit of using capitals as small capitals
grew, and eventually small capitals became a separate font; italic and
roman began to work together and to belong to one design. Textura
continued to be used in North Europe and, together with roman,
italic and capitals, it joined in the disconnection from sizes defined
by the human writing hand. Civilité appeared on the scene as well,
but did not share in the size disconnection. Greek type was made on
a large scale. Italic capitals were invented. Real display types were
made by Van den Keere: this means they had display proportions,
not just a large appearing size. (See chapter 19 for some discussion of
this.) Design proportions began to be defined for economic reasons,
not just aesthetic ones. Bolder and narrower types appeared; descenders became shorter, ascenders brisker, and x-heights more generous.
Arabic type was made for the Vatican Press.

Pierre Haultin continued, together with Granjon and Van den
Keere, to make large x-height types or to revise existing ones. Haultin,

after setting the size limit for the roman, set a limit for its width as well [10.2]. It was a long time before this type was beaten in efficiency. Haultin also used a 'right-size capital' together with his lowercase. His capitals were much smaller and lighter in weight than was then usual, without any loss of readability.

The subsequent development of type has its roots in the fact that the punchcutters from this period knew their trade. They knew that steel provides another kind of accuracy from that of the writing hand. And they knew also that the limits of type are not determined by levels of technique, but depend on the limits of our nervous system: which are the same today as four hundred years ago. The punchcutters provided the printer – themselves, in most cases – with these materials because they had the skill, technique, and vision to make them not because somebody else wanted them to make type or because skilled calligraphers gave them designs to execute. If this happened occasionally, it should be regarded as an exception rather than the rule. Soon for both printers and punchcutters the reference point was not manuscripts but rather the work of a more successful competitor printer. Punchcutters began to imitate punchcutters and not scribes.

In this period, as well as an increase in the sizes of type, a rudimentary standardization of body sizes was developed. One could better describe it as a standardization of line increment (the concept of 'leading' did not yet exist). This standardization could not yet use a fundamental unit, such as would later be developed in France. Rather this standardization went under names, different in each European language. In English: Nonpareil, Minion, Brevier, Bourgeois – up to Canon. These names stood for a size of body, but were at the same time used to define the size of the appearing image. Body size was already then regarded as separate from letter image. This can be simply seen in the letter images as well as in the size-names in the very few type specimens that survive from this period. For example 'Reale' is a type made to fit onto a Reale body, which gives 11 lines over 65 mm [10.3]. 'Parangonne sur la Reale' is a type made originally

Reale Romaine.

Anachar. Scytha. Aiebat fe mirari quî
fieret, vt Athenienfes qui prohiberent
mentiri, tamen in cauponum tabernis
palàm mentirentur . Qui vendunt
merces, emuntque lucri caufa , fallunt
quemcunque poffunt, quafi quid pri-
uatim effe turpe , fiat honeftum , fi pu-
blicè facias in foro. At in contractibus
maximè fugiendum erat mendacium.
Sed tum maximè mentiuntur homi-
nes, quum maximè negant fe mentiri.

65 mm

10.3
*The name here indicates a particular size of body, and thus a particular line
increment: 11 lines of this 'Reale' are about 65 mm deep. (Plantin's* Index
characterum, *Antwerp, 1567.)*

Parangonne sur la Reale.

Anachar. Scytha. Percontanti quæ naues eſſent tutiſſimæ, Quæ, inquit, in ſic-
cum protractæ ſunt. Solebant enim olim
naues ijs menſibus, quibus mare nauiga-
bile non eſt, machinis quibuſdam in ſic-
cum pertrahi. Anacharſis ſenſit, omnem
nauigationem eſſe periculoſam. At ille de
genere nauigij percontabatur. Sunt enim
Liburnicæ, onerariæ actuariæque naues,
aliæque diuerſi generis, in quibus alia eſt
alia aduerſus tempeſtatem inſtructior.

10.4
*'Parangonne sur la Reale' means that the image of the type has the size of
'Parangon', but is then cast on 'Reale' bodies. With this practice, letter image
(type design) comes to be seen independently from size of body. (Plantin's*
Index characterum, *Antwerp, 1567.)*

to fit a Parangon body (10 lines over 65 mm) but cast in this case on the Reale body [10.4]. Typography had by then matured much more than we usually acknowledge. Those terms served their purpose well enough: perhaps better than when we now say '12 on 16 point', which sounds more precise than it is.

All this happened in the period that opened when Antoine Augereau passed on his knowledge to his apprentice Garamond, up to the time when Granjon, Van den Keere and the first Guillaume Le Bé died: between, let us say, the years 1520 and 1600.* This period was so rich in the development of typographic material, in quantity as well as quality, that afterwards nothing new was needed for another hundred years. If something new was made, it could not compete with already available material. So, after 1600, we often see damaged characters in a font being replaced by clumsy new ones. Much effort was put into illustration, rather than into type. Thus Hendrik van den Keere's son Pieter ended up as an engraver of maps, not a punchcutter. And since there was no need for new type, the punchcutters lost the position they enjoyed from the close connection between printing and the wider cultural sphere. Other forces began to take over. Soon the punchcutter became a person who only executed the designs or wishes of other people.

The best known case of the separation of design from execution is the 'romain du roi'. Here, in France at the end of the seventeenth century, intellectual reason struggled in a dialogue with practice and human limitations. An academic committee – the Académie Royale des Sciences – investigated the very down-to-earth processes of designing and making type. The results of the research were published as sets of plates, showing letters apparently determined by pure geometry and a fine grid [10.5]. The type that was made from

* The story of Garamond's apprenticeship to Augereau may rest on just one piece of evidence, but it makes sense. Such a passing on of knowledge between contemporaries and down the generations must lie behind the improvements of this time. See Carter's discussion: *A view of early typography*, pp. 83–6.

74

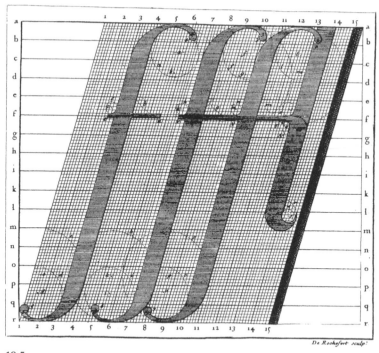

De Rochefort sculp.'

10.5

A concept diagram for the first true design for printing type. The punchcutter
followed the final form of this letter, though could not put any of this strict
geometry into practice.

these 'designs' could not of course follow the grid of the engraved
letters. And this allowed Fournier – who perhaps took more from the
Académie des Sciences than he wanted to acknowledge – to ridicule
the enterprise:

'The square they divide into 64 parts, each subdivided into
36 others, making a total of 2,304 little squares for roman capitals.
Italic letters are constructed by means of another square, oblong and
inclined, or rather a parallelogram, which undergoes a greater degree
of subdivision. Add to this numerous curves done with a compass;
for example, 8 for the a, 11 for the g, as many for the m, etc, and it will

be appreciated how useless is such a multiplicity of lines for shaping letters on a steel punch whose face, in the case of the letter most often used in printing, measures no more than the twenty-fourth part of an inch across.'*

It is not necessary to agree with Fournier's heroic conclusion that 'genius knows neither rule nor compass, save in mechanical work'.[†] But we can say that type constructed on a grid with the help of ruler and compass is only successful when executed by the designer himself, who will only use the grid to work faster, not to make things more rational and supposedly better.

So, with the demise of the independent punchcutter, style came back and influences from outside typography started to affect the form of letters. Contrast in the stroke-width of letters became gradually more pronounced, until it was not much more than a fashion item. There were a few exceptions, such as Kis, Fournier, and Bodoni. But the transformation of the punchcutter into a simple functionary continued. By 1900 there were very few punchcutters left, and most of these – for example Edward Prince in England – were skilful executors of other people's designs. The machine age, in the form of the pantograph and mechanical typesetting, was beating against the door of hand-work. By the 1920s, the whole process of type manufacture had been taken into mass production, and was carried out under factory conditions.

* Carter, *Fournier on typefounding*, pp. 7–8.
[†] Carter, *Fournier on typefounding*, p. 9.

Punchcutting in the sixteenth century

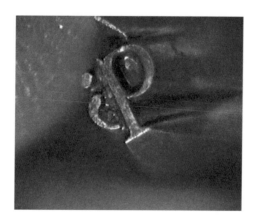

A real beauty this q́; (standing for the abbreviation 'que' and frequently used
in Latin). It was specially cut by Garamond, for reasons of economy, for this set
of punches. And in this way he could also kern the combination of q and the semicolon. Here we see three different techniques used within one punch. The accent
is entirely made by means of small files, simply filing away the material around it.
The q itself is made with a counterpunch, for its counter, and with the help of files
for the outer contour. The space between the q and the semicolon is dug away
with gravers. The tracks made by the gravers are clearly visible.

11 Punching and digging

In brief: there are two different approaches or traditions in punch-cutting. There is the tradition of counterpunching and cutting; and there is the tradition of digging and cutting. Both methods treat the outer contour in the same way: filing and then cutting. The essential difference between these two approaches is that the former uses counterpunches and the latter does not.

The main problem in making punches lies in the counters of a character. The digging method is to dig these shapes out. In German the tool that does this is a 'Grabeisen', which, translated literally, means 'digging iron': a name that illustrates perfectly how and with what purpose the tool is used in the digging approach. The English name for the same tool is 'graver'. In Flemish and Dutch it is 'steker' ('stabber' in English).

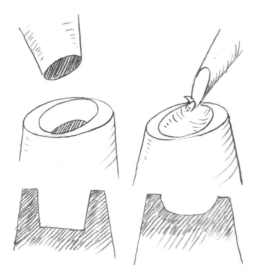

11.1

The two approaches to making the counters of letters. Striking a counterpunch into the punch (left); and digging with a graver (right).

In the counterpunching approach, these counters are themselves first made as punches (the so-called counterpunch), which are then struck into another piece of steel, from which the actual punch is made. One can find vigorous condemnations of the digging method – and advocacy of counterpunches – in the writings of authorities such as J. G. I. Breitkopf, J. M. Fleischman, Johannes Enschedé; and Fournier too makes his preference for counterpunches clear (see chapter 13).

It is not clear how old the discussion is between these two approaches, but probably it is as old as pre-typographic punchcutting. Benvenuto Cellini, in his text on goldsmithing of around 1560, advises the use of counterpunches. And certainly the early punches left to us (from the period 1520–1600, by Guyot, Garamond, Tavernier, Granjon, and Van den Keere) clearly show the use of counterpunches. The use of a counterpunch is not just a way of working, but also represents a view of what the letters should be. It suggests an unspoken design awareness, of a kind that has only become articulated in words and diagrams in recent years.

When one considers type design as a whole process, it becomes clear that working with counterpunches brings only advantages. One of the most important advantages is that you can use certain counterpunches for more than one character. An obvious example is the counter in the lowercase characters d, b, p, and q. These counters should be the same, to a very large extent. So you can make all these counters with only one counterpunch. But working in the other tradition, you have to dig out the same counter (more or less) four times. This is less accurate and takes much more time than making one counterpunch and hitting it once into each of the four punches.

Then suppose the cutter spoils a punch. In this case he only has to hit the counterpunch again, and half the work is done. So counterpunches enable the punchcutter to repeat shapes in a very quick and accurate way. And the repetition of shapes is a fundamental factor in type design. There are further advantages too, which are suggested in my discussion of Fournier (chapter 13).

Some people also maintain that counterpunches do not give neat counters. A counterpunch is made in just the same way and with the same materials and tools as a punch itself, so accuracy and sharpness of line are exactly the same. When you hit the counterpunch, you just have to make sure that you hit it straight down, otherwise you get a shape you don't want. Hitting counterpunches is a problem easily solved. When a hardened counterpunch penetrates the soft unhardened steel, the counterpunch shape is copied into the punch itself. There is absolutely no loss, just as there is no loss either when a punch is hit into a piece of copper, in order to produce a 'strike' (an unjustified matrix).

Using counterpunches thus brings many advantages, not only for general type-design technique, but also for the mundane but important factors of accuracy, time-saving and general efficiency in work. With a good set of counterpunches, punchcutters could work fast and with consistency. In other words, it brought some system into the work. One can compare this system with the early and very primitive hinting systems that we used some years ago in digital type design.

So where does the digging approach come from? Why has it been used by some of the twentieth-century punchcutters? For example this was the method said to be in use at Enschedé, under the regime of Van Krimpen and Rädisch. In a note to his edition of Fournier of 1930, Harry Carter writes: 'In Germany, where alone the art of letter-cutting by hand still flourishes, the modern school condemns counterpunching as unworkmanlike ...'.* And in a note to their edition of Moxon's *Mechanick exercises*, published first in 1958, Carter and Davis write that 'the surviving German school prefers to dig out counters with engraving tools'.† This reference to 'German' is confusing. Certainly the punchcutters still practising at the Imprimerie Nationale prefer to dig with engraving tools.

* Carter, *Fournier on typefounding*, p. 29; and p. 96 below.
† Moxon, *Mechanick exercises*, p. 109.

It is not clear exactly when the school of punchcutting at the Imprimerie Nationale started: perhaps in the mid-nineteenth century. But, as far as I know, it is the only training in the craft that has been developed into a real discipline, passed down from master to pupil, over several generations. The common way had been for each punchcutter to develop his own methods, and sometimes to pass these on to another person. For example, Antoine Augereau taught the essentials of punchcutting to Claude Garamond, and Dirk Voskens probably did the same for Nicolas Kis. But more usually, when the punchcutter died, his knowledge and the standards he had achieved over a lifetime went with him. For example, Hendrik van den Keere died without a real successor, although his business was one of the first real typefoundries, and a flourishing one too.

At the Imprimerie Nationale, however, a certain method of work has been refined over several generations, in calm and now rather academic circumstances. The result is an extraordinarily high level of skill and mentality. The digging approach used there is understandable when you have to cut the complex shapes of non-Latin characters. It is questionable when you are working on the simple and repetitive shapes of the roman alphabet. But, again, digging is understandable when any views about type that the cutters may have do not matter, and when their only aim is to put their skill at the service of strict specifications made by somebody else. This reaches fantastic extremes in the cutting of facsimiles of historic punches – copying every fracture or blemish – so that new matrices can be made and 'historic' type can be cast, without risk to the original punches. The results are astonishing – and successful.

Whichever country it belongs to, the digging method is in my view an inferior technique, under the following conditions: first, for the making of roman type; and, second, when the punchcutter is working without any strong specifications. In other words, when the punchcutter is also the designer. There is evidence to suggest that some of the early punchcutters, such as Garamond and Granjon, sometimes used digging methods. But their use of it was inconsistent.

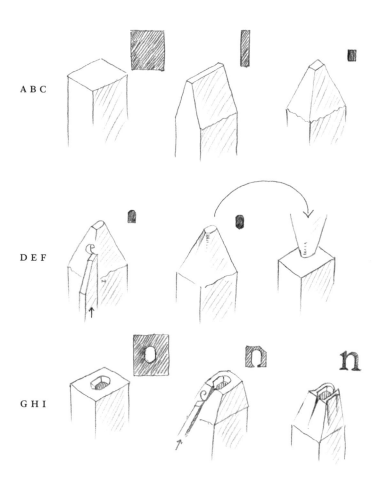

11.2

Stages in making a punch: the punchcutter starts out by making a counter-punch from a piece of steel, square in cross-section (A); the steel is quickly shaped with crude files (B, C); when the counterpunch is nearly finished, the shape can be fine tuned with gravers (D); the finished counterpunch is then hardened and struck into another piece of (unhardened) steel (E, F); the counterpunch leaves its impression, a hole that will become the counter of the punch itself (G); crude files are used to remove superfluous material from the punch (H); the final punch shows the mirror image of the letter (I).

And I am almost sure that Van den Keere did not use the digging technique when it was not necessary to do so, for example in very complicated characters, such as civilité capitals. It is too close to general engraving techniques; and there is an essential difference between punchcutting for type and engraving.

The sixteenth-century punchcutter supplied a product whose final purpose was to print: to give a two-dimensional image. But in making punches, the punchcutter had to think about letters three-dimensionally. In this respect, the punchcutter is nearer to a sculptor than to someone who can draw neat 'typographic' letters. An engraver,

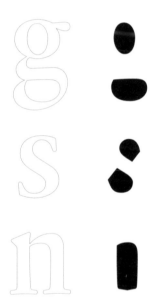

11.3

The difference between the two approaches can also be seen as a difference of mentality. A 'digger' works with an outline drawing at the back of his mind. A 'counterpuncher' works with shapes and surface areas. Sixteenth-century punchcutters certainly mixed the two techniques; but the counterpunch method provided a sure basic approach.

however, has much more in common with a draughtsman than with a punchcutter – let alone a sculptor.

In much of the literature of the subject, these terms of engraver and punchcutter are often confused with each other. Punchcutters are called engravers, although engravers are never called punchcutters. This is certainly so in English, in which much of the literature is written; but the same mistake is probably made in other languages. We often read that the punchcutter 'engraves' punches. But – certainly in modern English usage – this should be 'cuts', not 'engraves': unless the punches are really being dug into.

Putting things very crudely, one can say that an engraver aims to dig out a contour neatly. A punchcutter makes shapes and checks them over; these shapes are surfaces and not contours or outlines. And these surfaces demand to be considered three-dimensionally. Warren Chappell is a rare case of somebody who understood this enough to write a few words about 'the sculptural aspect of punchcutting'.* But then he had done a little punchcutting himself, as a student of Rudolf Koch. Consider again, in this light, the process of making a piece of type. This architectural and sculpting aspect becomes clear. The chapter that follows emphasizes it further.

* Warren Chappell, *A short history of the printed word*, New York: Alfred A. Knopf, 1971, p. 46.

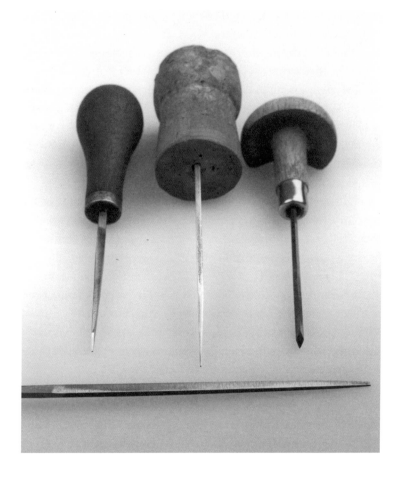

12.1
*Some gravers shown at true size. On the left: made from an old file, square tip,
medium size. In the middle: round tip, medium size, with a champagne cork
handle. Right: oblique tip, large, and a more conventional handle. At the bottom:
a file, square in section, its working edge pointing towards us. The shiny edge
(and its reverse side) is made smooth for filing action as it passes between the
fingers. The champagne cork is a tip from Christian Paput: such handles are very
comfortable, pleasant to acquire, and simple evidence that every punchcutter
adapts and invents his own tools and methods of working.*

12 The delights of steel

Punches are made of steel. The word steel makes most people think of hard, heavy, cold, stubborn, and tough material. The properties just listed are certainly not pleasant and usually they are considered negative. Despite the fact that punches are made of steel, in punchcutting practice these negative characteristics are hardly encountered when cutting for text sizes.

A punch is first a little bar of steel, relatively light in weight, and, in relation to its size, its weight is pleasant. The main part of the steel that has to be removed is taken off quickly and fairly easily with a large crude file. After this is done, small fine files are used to shape the punch and image roughly. These fine files are put aside the moment they become too crude and when there is a danger of removing too much steel. The final cutting of the letterform can then be made with a graver.* This is no more than a little thin bar of hardened metal with a straight, negative or even a positive cutting angle. This is inserted into a handle. The cutting edge of a graver can have any shape: whatever helps you to make the letter-shape you want.

The punchcutter's graver is not the elegant and expensive engraver's burin that can still be bought today. The punchcutter's tool is much shorter than the engraver's: this gives more control in use. Plenty of them are needed, differing in cutting angle and shape. A graver is constantly altered, to perform different, particular tasks. You soften it, then reshape it by means of other gravers, harden it again and sharpen it. Then it is ready for use. All of this will take ten minutes or so. Changing a graver is necessary for special details in the design. In this way a punchcutter supplies himself with special curves and angles. In order to work correctly and pleasantly your graver has to be sharp. To test its sharpness, just put the graver on your thumb-

---

* But the punchcutters still working at the Imprimerie Nationale do not use gravers for fine tuning the outer shape. They always use very fine files for this.

nail. Without any pressure you feel it sinking a little into your naturally very sensitive thumbnail. If you can easily cut curls from the nail
of your thumb, then the graver is sharp enough.

If we put this graver against the punch at a certain angle, the
cutting edge will dig itself into the unhardened steel of the punch.
This happens as easily as it did in your thumbnail. With a very light

12.2
*A file in use. The file is rubbed to and fro, the guiding fingers on the smooth sides,
working from the shoulder of the punch upwards.*

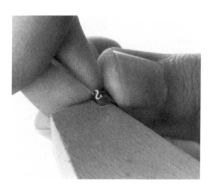

12.3
*The process of digging. A counter is altered with a graver, working from
the face of the punch downwards. The piece of wood is a 'tag', with incisions
in which to rest a punch.*

pressure – one can't call it effort – you push the graver upwards and by doing this you cut away a little curl of steel. Press a little more and these curls will become thicker. If you keep your hand steady you can cut away long curls too, even to a length of 3 mm. At moments like this, steel is no longer steel. It looks and feels much more like cold butter: there is the same ease, pressure and pleasure with which you cut off larger and smaller curls of butter with a knife. Then you feel nothing but delight in this substance, with such a strong and fine structure, which we call steel.

What is possible with a piece of steel and a graver? To gain an idea of the punchcutters' accuracy, we can attempt a comparison between their technique and our present techniques. The little curls of

12.4

The curls of steel cut by a graver. This electron microscope photograph shows an enlargement to 40 times real size. The horizontal line above 'OU' represents 100 mu (or 0.1 mm).

12.5

A further enlargement, from the centre of 12.4, to 300 times real size. The horizontal line still represents 100 mu.

steel cut off by a graver, as described above, are from 0.01 to 0.001 mm thick. I had these curls measured with an electron microscope [12.4, 12.5]. They are by no means the thinnest possible, but at least this information gives us some numbers and the possibility of making a comparison. So: 0.01 mm. How many dots per inch (dpi) is that? It is 2540 dpi. In other words, the punchcutter could easily work on the outline of type to at least the same accuracy as our high-resolution image setters.

    This comparison is very primitive. It should be expanded and well illustrated too. But numbers do not tell everything. They represent steps, and a punchcutter does not work in steps – any more than any living human being does. The punchcutter works by analogue, not digitally.

13 Fournier on punchcutting

The art of the punchcutter is this: to know the best possible shape that can be given to letters, and their proper relation to one another, and to be able to reproduce them upon steel so that they may be struck into copper to make the matrices by means of which the letters can ever after be cast in any numbers. *

A nice definition, although Pierre Simon Fournier in his *Manuel typographique* (1764) admits that 'the best possible shape of letters is a matter of personal taste and therefore it is not necessary to say more about this item'. About 'their proper relation to each other' he also says next to nothing. The letters have to be of the same size, they have to stand on the baseline, not too close nor too far from each other. His words are casual and not of great value for us. In his book, as elsewhere in such literature, there is little written about the essentials of type: the way it works, the differences and similarities between types. According to the translator and editor of Fournier, Harry Carter, our vocabulary is too limited. But nevertheless Fournier says some revealing things about 'reproducing letters upon steel'. His discussion, in conjunction with the necessary practical research, will help to take us a step further. First, of course, you have to read Fournier or at least the two chapters of his *Manuel* which deal with punchcutting. What follows here is chapters 2 and 3 of Harry Carter's edition of Fournier, with Carter's notes at the foot of pages. After this I have added some thoughts on what Fournier says: reference to these comments is given by numbers in Fournier's text, thus ▶1.

---

* Carter, *Fournier on typefounding*, p. 21. In reprinting this extract from Harry Carter's edition of Fournier, some very small changes in orthography have been made, for the sake of editorial consistency within our book. Carter's notes have been renumbered, to make one sequence.

THE FACE-GAUGE

The face-gauge[1] is a small piece of brass, sheet-iron, or tin, rectangular in shape, of the thickness of a card, on which are marked the heights which the letters should have: and this is a matter requiring much forethought. ▶1 To perform the work successfully I have devised the following method. I divide the body of the letter which I am to cut into seven equal parts, three for the short, five for the ascending and descending, and seven or the whole for the long letters. The ensuing sketch will sufficiently explain this.[2]

m a   M d   p q   j Q

These heights once fixed, it remains to mark them on the gauge. To do this I square the corners of the piece of brass which I select for the purpose: then mark the distances with a steel point, guiding it with an adjustable set-square. This set-square, also called a bevel, has one flat and moveable arm fastened by a screw into a thicker upright piece which overlaps, and against which the piece of brass is laid. I first draw a vertical line across the gauge to ensure that the letters shall be perpendicular, then with dividers set to the three, five, or seven parts of the body, I draw these widths across the whole width of the gauge. It then only remains to take out the little square of brass between the lines with a file, leaving in its place a notch or opening, which is the gauge. There will therefore be four openings on one side of the

---

1. An adjustable gauge is generally used.
2. Note that this is only an illustrative diagram, not a sketch of the gauge. If Fournier is thinking of an x as the standard lowercase letter, his proportions are the same as Caslon's.

piece of brass, that is to say, one of seven parts for the long letters, one of five for the ascenders and descenders, one of three
for the short letters, and one of three and a half for the small
capitals, since to look well these have to be a little bigger than
the other shorts. The ascending and descending letters, such as
d, h, y, are tested with two gauges, that of five parts for the whole
and that of three parts for the bowl or middle-part of the letter,
which should be on a level with the short letters. So much for
the roman letter.

The other side of the gauge is used for the italics. The horizontal lines for them are drawn at the same time as those for the
roman; it is only necessary to draw an oblique line from top to
bottom of the gauge to obtain the slope of the italics. But since
it is desirable that all the italic letters, big and small, should have
the same inclination, this must be marked once and for all upon
a piece of brass, which will serve as a gauge for this purpose. To
make this gauge, one corner of a piece of brass is squared and
another is cut to an obtuse angle, giving it the inclination which
it is desired to give to the italic. This little plate, called a standing italic gauge,[3] which is used as a standard for the inclination
of all the italics, is placed under the moveable arm of the bevel,
which is inclined to conform to it, thus giving the correct slope
to be marked on the gauge.

The gauge thus made with one side for the roman and the other
for the italic will serve for what is called ordinary face, which is that
in commonest use. If it is desired to cut a large face letter, which
means one in which the short letters are bigger (after the manner of the second one here shown [m m]) than those of the first

---

3. The normal slope is fifteen degrees or a little more. To look
right, 'pothook' strokes such as i must have a greater inclination
than the rest.

kind, the third opening in the gauge, which is for the short letters, is enlarged, or else the fourth opening, which was intended for the small capitals, is used instead. This shortens the ascending or descending parts of the d, q, etc, and makes their bowls by so much the bigger. The ascending or descending parts cannot be lengthened, because they would then exceed the body, which is always the same whether for large or small face. All that can be done is to make these ascending and descending letters fit more tightly into the second opening in the gauge, or even to enlarge this a little, which is permissible because the short letters of a large face taking up more space in the middle of the body, the ascenders begin lower and the descenders higher, which gives them both just a little additional height. ▶2

There is one point most necessary to be observed in cutting the gauge, which is to make the opening for the short letters a little smaller for the italic than for the roman. If they were made equal, the italic, when printed, would look bigger than the roman, since in point of fact a sloping line is longer than an upright one when the two occupy the same space.[4]

The gauges for other letters are cut in the same way according to their size and shape, which must be carefully attended to, since upon this depends what is called the scan of the letters.[5] A gauge, and more especially the part of it which is for short letters, made a little too big or too small will throw everything out. One letter measured singly may seem neither appreciably too big nor

---

4. This plan is seldom adopted. Italics are generally made lighter in colour instead. Fournier was attacked by a glossator of his Petition for making his italics too heavy: Bibl. Nat. Ms. fr 21117, no. 18.

5. i.e. their general effect. 'Scan' is an Americanism, which conveniently renders the French 'coup d'oeil'.

too small, but ten thousand composed into printed matter repeat
the error ten thousand times over, and, be this never so small, the
effect will be the opposite of what was intended. The same trouble also occurs when a stroke is made either too thick or too thin
relatively to its length, which makes a letter look clumsy and
faulty, without the reason for it being always easy to find out.

The size of the letters being thus fixed by the gauge, the punches must be cut accordingly.

PUNCHES AND COUNTERPUNCHES

The punch is the letterform cut on a bar of steel. For making it
a piece of steel should be chosen of good quality and of a size
suitable for the work to be done upon it. It should be clean and
without flaws: German steel is to be preferred to English, the latter being too fine and brittle for this kind of work.[6] ▶3

To make the punch we begin with the counterpunch,[7] which
gives the shape of the inside part of the letter. This shape must
first of all be cut on a little bar of steel, the right way round as it
will appear on the paper. Here are some examples side by side
with the letters: ·e ꞁ E ꞁ a ꞁꞁ m ꞙ M · d · h. Some of the counterpunches serve for several letters: ▶4 this shape ·, for example,

---

6. English cast steel is the invariable medium, even in Germany:
Prechtl's *Technologische Encyklopädie*, Stuttgart, vol. 16 (1850),
p. 395; Bachmann, *Die Schriftgiesserei*, Leipzig, 1867, p. 19. Fournier's method of hardening was too drastic for a fine steel.
7. Observe that many counterpunches make more than one dent
in the punch, e.g.: A, E, a, e, s, ffl. Parts of the counterpunch
have therefore to be cut away with files or gravers, or dented
with a counter-counterpunch.

will do for b, d, p, q, and this one ı for h, n, u. The same holds good for a few others. The letters with no central whites, such as i, I, ı, r, and others like them, need no counterpunch, the punches for them are cut with a file only. But in other cases they are a necessity; with other tools it would never be possible to hollow them out so uniformly and perfectly.[8] The perfection of the letter's shape depends upon the accuracy with which the counterpunch is made. To make sure that it is right, the punchcutter strikes it lightly into a piece of lead or type-metal. ▶5 After cutting away with a sharp penknife the burr due to the metal's being thrown up round the impression, he draws the letter outside it, with a steel point, then by testing it by the gauge in which the letter should fit he sees whether it is of the proper shape and size. ▶6 He enlarges, diminishes, or reshapes the counterpunch until he judges it to be correctly made for the letter to fill the appropriate measure in the gauge.

---

8. In Germany, where alone the art of letter-cutting by hand still flourishes, the modern school condemns counterpunching as unworkmanlike, on the ground that the uneven density of a punch so treated causes it to go out of shape in the striking. They dig out the counters with gravers. Old writers are unanimously of the opposite opinion, e.g. J. G. I. Breitkopf, in his *Nachricht der Stempelschneiderey und Schriftgiesserey* (1777) says (p. 8): 'Bad letter-cutters who do not properly understand the art of softening and hardening their steel cut the hollows inside the letters out of their punches with the graver only. But in this way the letters lose much of the fairness of their curves and the straightness of their stems. On the other hand, the man who knows his trade makes a counterpunch corresponding exactly to the interior of the letter, drives this once and for all into his punch, and finally cuts away the outside with files.' Equally emphatic were

When a number of counterpunches are made, they are hardened by heating and plunging, to enable them to act on the punches.

The punches are steel bars, cut to a uniform length, which is roughly two inches, softened by annealing them in a very hot fire. When they are of the same red as the fire, a cover is put over the furnace to damp it down and they are left to cool slowly inside.

There is another way of annealing steel to make it still softer and pleasanter to work, especially for ornamental pieces where the graver has to be used. The bits of steel are put in a crucible and the interstices are filled up with soot from a wood-fire; the lid is put on the crucible and tamped up with fire-clay, and it is then put in the fire, and, when it is thoroughly red, the fire is allowed to die down, so that it gradually cools. These operations make the steel softer and more malleable, and cause it to offer less resistance to the counterpunch or graver. Next, one end of the

---

Fleischman and Johannes Enschedé (*Proef van letteren*, 1768), and the author of the *Kurze doch nützliche Anleitung von Form- und Stahl-Schneiden*, Erfurt, 1754 (p. 73). Lesser authorities, Rowe Mores (Reed, *Old English letter-foundries*, p. 300) and De Vinne (*Plain printing types*, p. 15), were of the same opinion.

The chief advantage of counterpunching, that the counters are made deeper and therefore do not so easily fill with ink, only applies where old-fashioned presses with soft blankets are used.

English nineteenth-century 'modern' and 'old-style' types – the high-water mark of technical skill – are all cut with counterpunches. On the other hand, some very delicate types, Unger's 'fraktur' and Marcellin-Legrand's 'nouvelle gravure', were evidently done with gravers.

The cutting of 'fraktur' types, especially the capitals, with counterpunches presents great difficulties.

steel bar is squared with a file, and it is then put in a stake,[9] in the middle of which there is a square hollow about an inch and a half wide, in which the punch is firmly held by two screws. The counterpunch is placed above it[10] and beaten in with a hammer, making an impression which is the principal part of the punch.[11]

This impression or counter may well be one forty-eighth of an inch for small sizes of letter and proportionately deeper for larger sizes.[12] This is the rule which our former masters of the art observed for the depth of their counters and it has been considered sufficient, to judge by the fact that their letters have always been used with uniform success.

For some years past they have been cutting punches in Holland, the depth of whose counters is greater;[13] of course no harm comes of it, but neither does it offer any advantage. However, some persons have extolled this uncommon depth as a most necessary thing. They would be right if letters wore out like certain

---

9. This is not a necessary tool. A vice will serve, provided the lower end of the punch rests on something solid.
10. If the counter is small, the counterpunch is simply placed over the centre of the face and beaten in. The face of the punch must be at least three times as wide as the counter. If the area of the counter is considerable, such as that of a 12 point capital, a hollow should be chipped out of the punch with a little chisel, and the tip of the counterpunch rounded. This avoids the risk of the counterpunch 'skating' over the punch and making a dent larger than itself. Some punchcutters use a contrivance consisting of two 'stakes', one of which can be moved in two directions relatively to the other. With this they can fix the counterpunch in the right position over the punch and strike it without fear of its moving. It may be necessary to anneal the punch between the blows.

things which are fit for use so long as some parts remain; but that is not the case with type: it always keeps its depth of counter with the exception of a slight decrease of about the thickness of paper, which comes of the wearing down of the parts in relief, which, becoming rounded at the edges, lose their proper contour. That is why the letter is worn out, though the depth of counter is the same as it was at first but for that trifling difference. It follows that letters, whether more or less deeply cut, become worn out and are returned to the metal-pot in either case with their depth the same as when they were new, save only for this slight decrease which is not affected by the depth of the counter. A letter with unusual depth therefore lasts no longer than one with a sufficient depth.

But, they say, a letter whose counter is deep is less soon filled with ink than one which is shallower. The answer to that is a

---

11. Because the shape of the letter is determined by the shape of the counter. When gravers only are used, the punchcutter draws the letter on the face, sometimes coating it with Chinese white mixed with gum. It is possible to have the letter photographed onto the face (Thibaudeau, *La Lettre d'imprimerie*, p. 480), but it seems incredible that it can be worth while.

12. The depth of the counter must depend on its width. Caslon's pica lowercase o is about the depth Fournier mentions, and quite deep enough. Fertel in 1723 complained of the insufficient relief of contemporary French type. De Vinne (*Plain printing types*, p. 16) thought Fournier's depth justified Fertel's complaint.

13. In the advertisements to their specimens of 1744–1768 Messrs. Enschedé boasted that 'By means of counterpunches the letters [Fleischman's] have been cut much deeper than a punchcutter has ever before cut or attempted to cut them. Therefore our types will wear and can be used longer than others.'

well-known fact: namely, that the counter of a letter ought never
to become filled with ink. If this occurs, it is a proof that the ink
in question is muddy and therefore bad, because, if it cause the
letter to fill, it will also thicken the strokes, a thing which ought
never to be allowed in a printing-house. It is not right to blame
the letter for the fault of the ink, as is not uncommonly done;
hence I have thought fit to emphasize the point here.

I say, therefore, that the counters of small letters, those from
a nonpareil to a small pica or a pica, should be about one forty-
eighth of an inch deep – more if desired: the effect is the same.
I have given some of my types this abnormal depth to please
those who may care for it, though I myself regard it as useless.
Nevertheless, letters must be of the depth which I have mentioned, and larger ones deeper in proportion to their size; otherwise, the bottom of the counter being too nearly on a level with
the face, the paper, under pressure, might make the ink flow into
it and cause it to print, which would be a serious fault.

There is another thing against which the punchcutter should
guard, that is giving too much shoulder[14] to the letter, either inside with his counterpunch or outside with his file. This defect
gives the character an unsightly thickening as it wears down.

After making the hollow in the middle of the letter with the
counterpunch, the next operation is to clear away the metal
from the outside. In the first place a coarse file is used to fine
down the punch, and then the outline of the letter is worked up
with smaller files; the punch being rested meanwhile against a
small projecting piece of wood fastened to the bench.[15] Next,

---

14. As far as possible, the shoulder outside a punch should be
such that no part of the shoulder of the cast letter shall project
beyond its body. If the type has this projection the rubbing
requires great attention.

the punch is put in an angle-piece[16] two inches high, which is placed upon an oilstone in order to face the punch. This angle-piece is called a facer: it may well be of wood with an iron plate underneath to give it strength. The punch is placed in this angle-piece, always with the same corner foremost so that its relation to the stone may not vary, and is held firmly in the angle with the thumb of the right hand; then both hands work the punch and the tool together backwards and forwards over the stone. By continual rubbing in this manner the letter acquires a uniform, level, and polished face.

If the counterpunch, which is cut with a shoulder, is driven in too far, it makes too large an opening to suit the proper gauge of the letter. In such an event the surface must be filed or faced down bit by bit whilst the outline of the letter is filed away proportionately until the punch assumes its proper size, shape, and thickness of stroke. The size is tested by means of the gauge, and the thickness of stroke by means of a punch finished to the punchcutter's satisfaction, which he uses as a pattern, constantly comparing it with the new one at which he is working.

The letters m, M are the ones used as standards, the first for the lowercase and the second for capitals. It must be borne in mind that it is impossible to judge of the perfection of the punch without taking an impression of it, since the letters

---

15. This is a piece of hardwood projecting horizontally from the bench near eye-level. At the fore-end is a notch (or several notches of various sizes) in which the punch is held during the filing, Moxon calls it a 'tach'; now it is often called a 'pin'.

16. The facing-tool now generally used is shaped like this,

 the top being of brass, and the flat bottom of steel. Fournier's pattern would be equally good, if carefully handled.

are all cut in reverse, thus: Ɔ, ᗡ, Ǝ, ꟻ, and are apt to look differently when seen the right way round; besides which the pleasing polish on the steel deceives the judgement, so that a punch which appears excellent that way round may prove not to be so at all when printed. To obtain the impression, the punch is held in a candle-flame to heat it and remove any oil from the counter as well as a certain dampness caused by the coldness of the steel. It is then wiped with a cloth, and afterwards put into the smoke of the candle, from which it takes a coating of rich black: it is lightly pressed on a card, damped, or moistened with the breath, on which it leaves with perfect sharpness the black with which it was coated. ▶7 Being now the right way round, the letter can be judged as perfect or faulty.

There being always something to be corrected after the first impression, the excessively thin strokes are strengthened by facing the letter on the stone, and reducing the others with a file. Should the inside of the letter need enlarging, the parts which need cutting back are taken off with a little hard-tempered steel tool, pointed and sharp edged, called a knife-file. The point should not project much more than a quarter of an inch from its handle to give it the more strength. I have been best served for this purpose by the half of a little English file, called half-round, which measures about an inch in length. These little files are extremely hard-tempered and easily break: the broken end is inserted in a handle with a long ferrule and held there with sealing-wax; the pointed end is sharpened and edged on the stone. By these means the punch is gradually given its proper shape, size, and gracefulness.

Greek, Hebrew, Syriac, Arabic, and other kinds of letter are cut in the same way, except for alterations in the cut of the gauge, which varies with the nature of the characters. Hebrew, for example, has no capitals and consists simply of small letters, a few of which have strokes descending slightly below the line. It is a fat and heavy letter, leaving little space between the lines. The lowercase Greek, on the other hand, is only half the size of Hebrew of the same body, because, like the roman character, Greek has capitals and short, ascending and descending, and long letters of several descriptions. The same is true of other Oriental alphabets, which are of various shapes and sizes. The punchcutter must seize the spirit and style of the letter which he has to cut in order to make the cut of his gauge fit it discerningly, for the reasons which I gave on an earlier page.[17]

As to the best possible shape to give to letters, it is useless to write of it: it is a matter for the taste and discernment of the cutter, and it is in this that he displays his proficiency or his incapacity. It is a safe rule that he should do nothing without a correct understanding of the design of the letters, or having good models before him to allow him to catch the fashion of them, and to make such alterations as he thinks necessary. For example, such an alteration has lately been made in the case of capital letters, whose angles have been squared to give an effect of lightness, whereas they were formerly somewhat concave, which gave the letters a heavier appearance. The same thing has been done to all the angles of the lowercase letters. ▶8

---

17. See above p. 94.

▶1 (p. 92)

The gauge that Fournier describes is a possible option. But in practice it is quite hard to make, cumbersome, not very accurate and not necessary either. Another way, for example, is to make punch-like pieces of steel. These have the same shape as a punch, but there is no letter on them, just a square or a rectangle [13.1]. You make one such gauge for the x-height, one for the cap-height, as well as one each for the ascenders and descenders. These gauges have the following advantages. You can make smoke-proofs of the gauge and compare these with the smoke-proofs of the punch. It is far easier to make these than it is to make Fournier's device. They can also be made to size much more accurately. In fact you have the same accuracy as that of punchcutting itself, since these gauges are made with the same tools and material and in the same way as the actual punches. Punch and gauge can be compared simply by holding them next to each other. Size is then measured very accurately by putting the faces against each other and holding them up to the light. In this position you can check the slope of the shoulder as well [13.2]. This method of measurement is as old as mankind itself and was put out of use only when microscopes were invented. Fournier's gauge is an academic one: it is logical and easy to follow, but in practice there are other and better methods. Each punchcutter would have had his own habits and variations.

13.1

On the left – a punch-like gauge. On the right – a diagram of its face, showing three measurements: x-height, ascender and descender length. The nick gives orientation to the baseline. A gauge such as this can be hardened and stands up to frequent use.

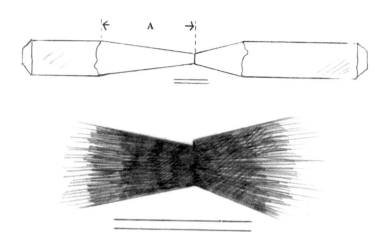

13.2

Using a punch-like gauge (left) also makes it easy to see whether the angle of the punch's shoulder needs refinement: the punch can now be shaped to follow the angle of the gauge's shoulder (A).

The design proportions that Fournier gives for a normal roman are rough and general: x-height 3, ascenders 2, descenders 2. In practice, punchcutters followed their own sense of what was right. There are plenty of examples that differ from the proportions suggested by Fournier. Here it feels as if he was writing with beginners in mind.

▶2 (p. 94)

This is a strange passage. Fournier talks here about cutting a face with an x-height larger than that for which its body was intended. He refers constantly to his gauge. It needs to be adapted. The x-height is enlarged, but the ascenders and descenders have to be reduced, or else they will stick out of the body. So the x-height enlargement is at the cost of those reductions above and below. Fournier is not clear about this. Apparently there were no general assumptions about these proportions then, though now we tend to make descenders smaller than ascenders. Fournier seems to imply here that if you want a typeface with a relatively larger x-height, you have to recut the lowercase letters entirely. But we know that this problem was solved in the sixteenth century: simply by casting a face made with, for example, a 10 point punch on a 9 point body. The only punches that had to be recut were those with ascenders and descenders. This was commonly done by Plantin and probably others too. Fournier does not mention it.

▶3 (p. 95)

As argued in chapter 10, the years between 1520 and 1600 mark the key period in punchcutting and type design. Alas, we know next to nothing about the metallurgic knowledge of that time. I suppose that much was never recorded. Many people knew things that they found no reason to write down, if they could write at all. Knowledge was transferred by doing, showing and talking. Much knowledge will have disappeared and will have been rediscovered later.

It is carbon that makes steel into what it is. You can influence the amount of carbon in steel. Benvenuto Cellini had already explained how to do this. So punchcutters had different kinds and qualities of steel available to them. The English cast steel that Harry Carter recommends was an eighteenth-century invention, and so not available to the early punchcutters. Today I use C-45. The number 45 stands for a certain amount of carbon in the steel. This is a standard and it does not matter much where the material comes from. However, it is rather tough. The twentieth-century Enschedé tradition recommends Huntsman Yellow Label. The tradition still active at the Imprimerie Nationale uses leftovers from a very old supply. Experienced punchcutters seem not to like working with the current standard material. As Christian Paput says, 'steel nowadays is not made to be worked by hand'.

We should not forget the character of craft workers. It is in their interests to keep knowledge to themselves. In those days even a medical doctor kept knowledge to himself: this was the proof that he was better than his competitor. The real knowledge, necessary for a certain kind or level of quality, will never be given free. It is there for the person who is, in the master's view, his follower and successor. But if the master were to be killed in a fight or to die through illness, then the knowledge was gone.

Another fact to bear in mind is that a good deal of this knowledge just cannot be stated verbally. That everything can be made clear through words is a very short-sighted and perhaps recent idea. Thus, when the pupil has reached a certain level of experience, the master will not explain but literally *show* him something. Some-times the pupil understands it in a flash. Sometimes not, and in that case the master will wait for some time to pass before trying again. All the while, master and pupil are surrounded by others who do not really understand (yet) what they are doing. But they work in a workshop and products have to be made. For these reasons highly skilled craft workers are often difficult people to deal with. Their skill does not depend at all on bookish education, intelligence or vocabulary.

▶4 (p. 95)

Here Fournier says something of great interest: 'Some of the counter-punches serve for several letters'. He means that you can use counter-punches for several different characters. He also implies that counter-punches should be carefully kept for their reuse. Alas he has nothing to say about when the counters are good enough and what their rela-tion is to each other. Further, Fournier says that a number of letters, such as i, I, 1 or r, do not need counterpunches. In theory, Fournier is right. However, his predecessors did use counterpunches for char-acters like these. If you use counterpunches here, you not only work faster but with greater precision too. This is because the counter-punch represents the right stem width.

For example, take capital T. The drawings here show a typical punch [13.3]. The little plateaux are made by the counterpunch. They wouldn't be there otherwise: it is almost impossible to make them without a counterpunch. Further, these little edges are quite useless. The counterpunch by which they are made can be deduced. This counterpunch is made, in turn, with a counter-counterpunch. This

punch would have been used for making several counterpunches and
it resembles the main stem width of the capitals. So, with the use of
one counter-counterpunch, the stem width of most of the capitals
is determined. As argued in chapter 11, this way of working is easy,
certain and quick. You don't have to search for the stem width of each
new capital letter. One finds these details on many sixteenth-century
punches: of capitals and also of some lowercase characters like r or f
[13.4].

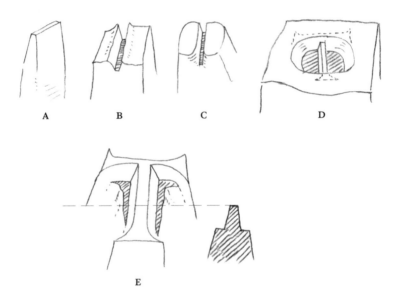

13.3

*A counter-counterpunch (A), a counterpunch (B, C), and the punch itself (D, E).
The counter-counterpunch is used to define the width of the stem of the T, and
is hit into the counterpunch. This counterpunch is then given its proper shape,
is hardened, and is then hit into the punch itself. Then the outer contour of the
punch is defined.*

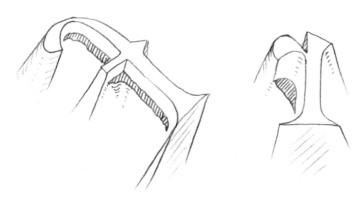

13.4

Some typical plateaux left by counterpunches. An experienced punchcutter will probably use the same counterpunch for f and for an fl ligature. For the r, an n counterpunch may have been reused.

►5 (p. 96)

The next point is Fournier's description of how he tests his counterpunch. He strikes it into a piece of type-metal, cuts away with a knife the resulting burr (the metal thrown up), and scratches with the tip of a knife the outside contour of the character around the hole made by the counterpunch. This is very unlikely. To test a counterpunch one does indeed hit it into a piece of soft metal; Benvenuto Cellini told us this also. However, to scrape or cut the burr away with a knife is a crude way of working: too crude for punchcutting. By doing this it is possible to deform in various ways the hole made by the counterpunch. If you want to have an exact image of the counterpunch, the burr has to be polished away. You face down this piece of metal just as you face down a punch itself.

Fournier mentions an exact depth of strike (pp. 98–100), and so might lead us to believe that one can drive in a counterpunch to just the right depth. Of course this is impossible. When you hit a counterpunch into the much softer type-metal, you always hit it too deep, and you do this on purpose. Fournier is not very specific about this.

You hit the counterpunch with one blow as straight as you can. It is impossible to hit a counterpunch exactly to a depth of say 1.5 mm, and even if you could do this it wouldn't help, because you are not looking for the right depth but for the right shape and size. That is somewhere on the counterpunch, but where exactly, you do not know.

▶6 (p. 96)

Fournier goes on to say that after he has hit the counterpunch into the type-metal and has scraped off the burr, he scratches with a steel point the outside contour of the letter, around the hole of the counterpunch. In this way he can look at a complete character. This sounds reasonable. And maybe just because of its air of reason, he wrote it down. Maybe Fournier worked like this for larger sizes, but it is very unlikely that he could have done so for the smaller sizes. Here too different solutions are possible. For example, it is possible to stab away the material around the counter, as a copperplate engraver does to achieve a reliable result. Although working in soft material, as here, this still takes a good deal of time. In my view, experienced punchcutters did test counterpunches, checking height, width and the relation of the counters themselves, as described below; but they did not take the trouble to scratch, engrave and draw, to get a reliable sketch in soft metal. They would not have done this because making a really good sketch takes almost as much time as making the actual punch, and the fact that the sketch has been executed in soft metal hardly helps speed the process.

In practice you do not draw or scratch at all. In reality smoke-proofs were made. A counterpunch always has a tapering shape: the result of facing down a piece of this type-metal is that the inverted shape made by the counterpunch gradually grows smaller and smaller [13.5]. One always hits too deep: so one always makes a hole that is too big. For this reason alone the image made by the counterpunch in the type-metal can be made smaller but not larger. (If you want to enlarge the image, then you have to re-strike.) Smoke-proofs are made from the piece of type-metal. The exact shape of the counterpunch

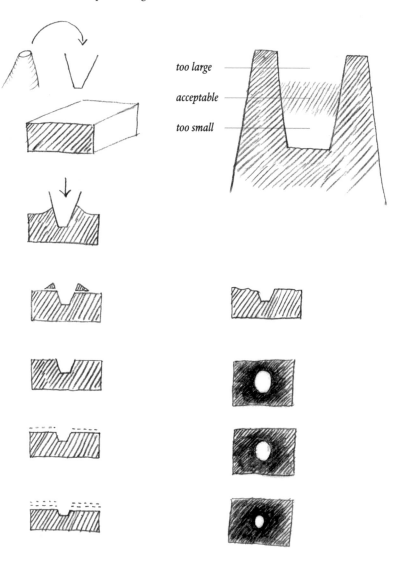

too large

acceptable

too small

13.5

A counterpunch is hit into a piece of soft metal (tin or type-metal), in order to check and correct its shape before the process of hardening and hitting into the punch takes place. The more you face down a counter made with a counterpunch, the smaller it becomes.

is seen in the white unprinted area. Now we can really check the height and other aspects as well, such as the width and curves of the counterpunch. The right shape is somewhere on the counterpunch and the punchcutter does not know where exactly [13.6]. Hitting the counterpunch in type-metal was a way of checking the shape of the counterpunch at different stages of its length. When a smoke-proof was judged correct, it was compared to other smoke-proofs of the same kind, but resembling other counters. But if you scrape away the burr with a knife you can't make a smoke-proof, because the surface is not even. And if you go on scratching the shape of the character with the tip of a knife, you will accidentally slip into the counter hole itself or end up pushing metal back into the hole. And so you destroy the shape made by the counterpunch in the type-metal. The method that Fournier describes is not usable for sizes up to at least 24 points.

To compare the counters with each other, to see how well they harmonize, it is of course necessary first to cut all the counterpunches: for example, counterpunches needed for the lowercase roman letters

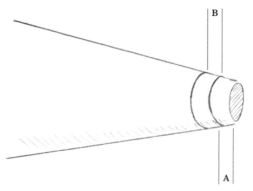

13.6

Like most other punches, a counterpunch is slightly tapered. So the deeper it is hit, the larger the counter will be. (Facing down the punch itself gradually decreases the size of the counter.) The punchcutter needs first a certain depth (A). Beyond this lies the area in which acceptable counters can be found (B). And further on is the zone in which counters are definitely too large for the typeface we are making.

or for the capitals, at any one size. Fournier does not say this, or if he does, he is very unclear. One gets the impression that this information is not very important for him. His words are: 'When a number of counterpunches are made, they are hardened by heating and plunging, to enable them to act on the punches.' But this number is, in practice, a very specific number: namely all the counterpunches you need for one set of characters [13.7]. An experienced punchcutter would have done this, so that he could look first at all the counters without worrying or being distracted by the form of the complete characters. He was not worried by this – as we might be – because he realized that a good set of counterpunches will result in good complete characters. The other way round is – certainly for a punchcutter – impossible. So once the punchcutter was looking at a harmonious set of counters, only then did he start to worry about the other parts of the characters. Without observing this order, but making punch for punch – first an A, then a B, an S or a Z – the punchcutter would lose a lot of time in readjusting characters for weight and width. It is even possible that he would not know where to look. And then the punchcutter would find himself in an endless corridor of corrections.

▶7 (p. 102)

Having hit counterpunches into the pieces of metal that will become the actual punches, Fournier's advice is to make smoke-proofs of the punches. Good judgement depends on this, he says, because then one can see the letter: not shiny and mirror-image, but black-on-white and the right way round. This is indeed a good thing to do. But when he goes on to describe a remedy for one of the common mistakes, he gives us some very doubtful advice. If, according to Fournier, the thin parts of your punch are too thin, you have to face down your punch a little more. Then the thin parts will become thicker. Unfortunately, the thick parts will become thicker as well. Facing a punch down cannot be done just like that: not only does the whole image become fatter, but the counter will become smaller [13.8].

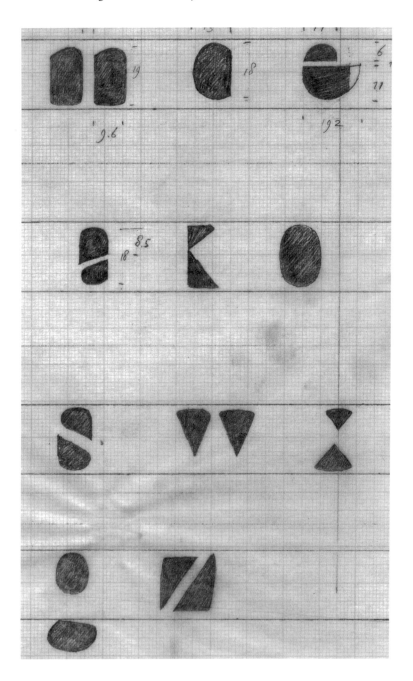

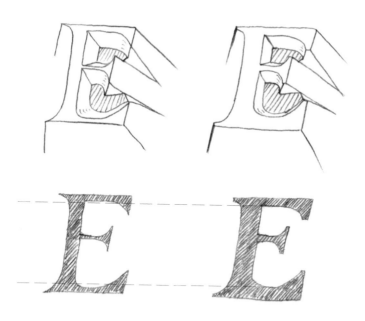

13.8

The effects of facing down a punch that is finished or nearly finished: all of the parts become thicker. But there is an unwanted consequence: the counter becomes smaller.

< 13.7

These are the basic counters for the roman lowercase character set. One can also see here how they relate – differently – to the x-height. The proportions of the counters are not fixed: they vary, and can sometimes be quite specific to a particular typeface design. Counterpunches are a great aid when fine-tuning the relations between these counters: they gain space and time for the punchcutter, quite literally.

Fournier goes on to say that if this happens, you enlarge the counter by cutting away with a knife-file. This advice is further evidence that punchcutters mixed the two techniques (as in the punch shown on p. 78). Fournier was of course no amateur, and why he gives us dangerous advice is not clear. Such knowledge is hard to put into words, and maybe the right words were too difficult for him: he constantly avoids essential issues. Maybe he was too much of a craftsman and so not completely generous with knowledge. But anyway his advice is misleading and disastrous for beginners.

If a punchcutter has this problem then he has given his counterpunch the wrong shape. It is a problem that should have been solved one stage before, when all the counterpunches are tested. That is why one makes smoke-proofs and tests the shape of a counterpunch at different levels. If you make a mistake and a counterpunch is indeed wrong, then you correct the counterpunch and not the punch itself. For example, in the punches for Van den Keere's Small Pica Roman, the counterpunch used to make the punch for d is then used a further nine times (b, p, q, and all their accented versions). I find it hard to believe that a punchcutter would fiddle around with a graver in the same counter ten times, to get them right and uniform. If a punch is wrong, it's scrap-metal – or good enough for some new counterpunch. Fournier's advice to dig into counters threatens all the balance and harmony you may have achieved. In fact it undermines the basis of the design.

▶8 (p. 103)

Fournier ends the chapter with some words about the style of letters. He distinguishes between a punchcutter skilled in cutting type (who needs no advice about style) and someone with technical skills but no experience in cutting or engraving letters. The novice in letters should do his best by following models. Then he mentions some current fashions, such as could be seen in the type and in the lettering of his day.

14 How did they really do it?

As discussed in chapter 11, there are two ways or traditions of cutting punches: the approach that uses counterpunches, and the one that digs out counters. Fournier was clear enough about his own use of counterpunches. But what about the great masters of the sixteenth century? I think that nearly all of them made use of the counterpunch technique, often in very clever and efficient ways; but they would have mixed techniques – choosing whichever technique was best for the problem to be solved. How can we know for sure? This question can be answered by looking at their punches.

At first I thought that a counter dug out entirely with gravers could not show the typical steep sides, flat bottom and the sharp corners (junctions) between the bottom (base) and the sides, which are so characteristic of the counterpunching method. It seems impossible to make these features with a graver [14.1].

A counterpunch always has a flat top. This is because a counterpunch is made just as the punch itself is. The punchcutter looks almost directly down on the counterpunch, at an angle of 70 or 80 degrees to it, and pushes files or gravers with an upward movement, from bottom to top. This top has to be flat, so that its surface works like a little mirror and thus gets a sharp contour too. This shiny flat surface is the punchcutter's only guide to the position of the counterpunch in his hand, his guide as to how and where he is making changes. If the counterpunch is without this flat top but is convex instead – as one might think was more logical – then the punchcutter doesn't see any clear shape and works in a hit and miss fashion [14.2]. So a counterpunch always has a flat top, and this results in a flat base to the counter in the punch itself.

James Mosley however pointed out to me that these assumptions should not be taken for granted. He arranged a visit to Paris, to talk with Christian Paput at the Imprimerie Nationale. Paput demonstrated that, using only gravers, it was his custom to make counters

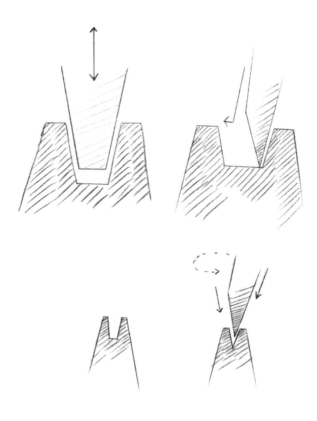

14.1
Above: The use of counterpunches (left) leaves punches with very deep counters.
In the digging method (right), the counters will be just deep enough.
Below: In a punch for a small size of type, it may be physically impossible for
the digging method (right) to make deep counters, let alone counters with
flat bottoms.

118

with steep sides, flat bottoms and a rather sharp angle between bottom and sides. He had learned from his master – had been trained
– to make the counters deep as well.

So this shattered my simple theory and raised my respect for
skilful engravers. But I still could not believe that the old cutters
worked entirely with gravers. It makes no sense, for several reasons.
I returned again to the historical punches in the Plantin-Moretus
Museum, and started to study more closely the complicated punches
where the cutter was tempted to mix techniques. The old punches
in the Museum provide evidence that is clear enough about this.
Whenever the digging method is used it can be clearly seen in the
tracks made by the graver. The picture on p. 78 shows the difference
in neatness between the dug-out part and the counterpunched counter. Punches like these are no exception and are found in the work
of many cutters. So it was not customary in the sixteenth century
to finish dug-out parts as neatly as the Imprimerie Nationale school

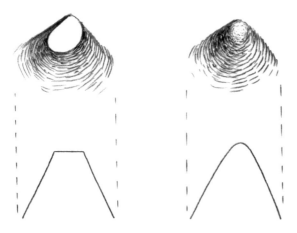

14.2
*When a punchcutter makes a counterpunch he makes sure that the top is flat
and shines like a mirror. Only then can the shape of the counterpunch be clearly
seen. If the counterpunch has a rounded top, all that the punchcutter sees is an
indistinct grey spot.*

still does today. The same remark goes for the plateaux on punches [13.3, 13.4]. Such neatness cannot have had any use. If there had been technical reasons to finish dug-out parts as nicely as the counter-punched parts, the punchcutters certainly would have done this. If, on the other hand, one supposes that both parts in such a punch were dug out, then it still makes no sense to finish one part neatly and not the other.

The second reason for me to believe that in the sixteenth century counterpunching was much used, and an effective method, is the fact that counters within one set of punches vary in depth. This is what happens if one uses counterpunches, because, as explained in chapter 13, the counterpunch bears the right image somewhere along its length and the punchcutter does not know exactly where [13.6]. The very skilful Christian Paput controls the depth of his counters and makes them not much deeper than is required for technical reasons. It is of course possible to dig out shapes and make them much deeper than is necessary: provided you are willing to invest time in a goal that has no use. However, I can imagine that the sixteenth-century counter had to be deep compared to the nineteenth-century counter, when printing equipment and processes could be much better controlled. But historical punches often show counters much deeper than is technically necessary. The punchcutters who made them worked on a contract basis and for them time was as valuable as it is for us.* Extra work was done at the punchcutter's own expense. So if counters were dug out, then they were certainly not dug out deeper than necessary. Take the punches shown on p. 42: the left m

---

* The biggest enemy of the maker is time. This is especially the case when highly cultivated skills and taste are fused together in one person. The writ-ings of creators and makers – whether historical or not, whether about paint-ing, music, drawing, sculpture, musical instruments, or anything else – have something in common: keeping up, or better, improving your personal stand-ards, within the scope allowed by economic necessity. If you do not succeed in that, then you might as well stop.

might have been dug out, but the one on the right certainly was not, and not only for the reason I have just given. Imagine the cutting point of a graver reaching for the bottom of that counter. There would not be much space left for the punchcutter to see what he was doing. He would have had to rely much more on what he felt than on what he could actually see. I simply do not believe that this digging happened. And no punchcutter ever mentioned it.

The last reason to believe that counterpunching was customary in the sixteenth century is this. Consider the number of identical counters that had to be cut to complete a roman set. For example in one set by Claude Garamond, the counter of the lowercase q appears ten times. It takes some time to cut a counterpunch and hit it ten times into another piece of steel. But it takes much longer to dig out ten equal counters.

The work still done at the Imprimerie Nationale proves that it is possible to make punches for type by digging out the counters. This too has to be understood historically. It was during the nineteenth century that the punchcutters definitely lost their independent position. Their skills were still very much in demand, but really only their skills. What was to be cut was largely defined by forces such as fashion, which no one could control. The foundries had grown larger too, and had become real businesses in which staying a step ahead of competitors could be crucial. These systems needed punchcutting skills on demand: one saw cutting benches in rows, with a punchcutter behind each of them. By this time too, type had begun to be drawn on paper: as a design to be implemented by an executor. This person could be a real typographic punchcutter, such as Edward Prince (who used counterpunches), or an engraver skilled in cutting tiny shapes of any description. P. H. Rädisch, originally a steel-engraver, would be an example of the second kind. When he began to execute Van Krimpen's designs, Rädisch had to teach himself how to cut punches for type. At the end of his career, he used photographic etching methods to transfer a design, reduced, onto a piece of brass or copper. A smoke-proof was made from this, and that was then pasted onto a steel bar.

Rädisch then did a skilful engraving job, using his previous experience of interpretation in the reduction of images, with commentary from Van Krimpen. Here, as in other such relationships in the twentieth century, the designer supplied the 'taste', the workman provided the execution skills. There is little connection between this and punch-cutting as it was done by someone like Granjon or Haultin. With the early punchcutters, design thinking and manual skills were fused into one process.

15 Fixing the image

However promising a punch or a smoke-proof may seem, this has little bearing on the way the letter looks when it takes its place between all the other letters in print. A whole process of work has to be done before one can print with the isolated design. First a punch has to be hit or pressed into softened copper, so that the image of the punch is exactly copied onto the piece of copper, without any loss. Now we have a strike, which is an unjustified matrix.

Justifying rough strikes is a crucial part of the process: it makes or breaks the actual design. In the early days of printing, justifying was probably done by the punchcutter himself. Later, when punchcutters became independent contractors cutting two or more designs a year, then other people were responsible for the task of justifying. The master-punchcutter's time was too valuable to be spent on such a time-consuming job. But, like a punchcutter, a justifier had to understand the principles of type design: he was a specialist, probably with a long training in his craft.

Justifying has to be done in all directions. The character has to be placed properly on the imaginary baseline, so the space above and underneath the character has to be adjusted accordingly. Then the space on either side must be defined, so that for all character combinations there is even inter-character spacing: to create a well balanced word-image, as discussed in chapter 4. But before all this can be done, the depth of the strike must be made equal to that of all the others. Without this, at the moment of printing, the faces of some types would be higher than others: some types would not print, others would get too much pressure. This equalling of depth means also that the image on the face of the type should lie exactly flat and parallel to the top of the matrix; otherwise, for example, only parts of a letter would be printed. So justifying matrices meant much more than simply defining space on either side of a character. Punches might carry letter images of the highest quality; but if the matrices

15.1
Justification is generally considered to be not much more than the correct placing of a character: horizontally and vertically within the character box that, for industrial reasons, provides the field of operations.

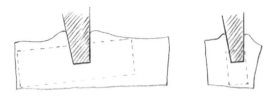

15.2
In the sixteenth century, justification really had to start from nothing. The strike (shown here in side and end views) was probably not much more than a lump of copper with one or two flat sides. Somewhere in this lump there floats a character. Justification in all directions was necessary.

124

are not justified properly, then all the work of cutting punches is ruined.

The matrix is then placed in an adjustable mould and type can be cast. The type is then freed of any casting excrescences on its body and is dressed to bring it to the right height. And, finally, the type can be composed and printed from. Anything can go wrong during the printing process: some areas may be inked too much, or get too little ink, or receive too much or too little pressure. The consequence: a page of uneven blackness. Every punchcutter would have been familiar with these possibilities and would have reckoned with them in some way during the cutting of punches, although no punchcutter could overcome or compensate for bad presswork.

In the literature of typography, hardly anything has been written about this essential part of the process of type design.* I would be interested in a thorough study of a design justified twice: once by its maker, once by a colleague or competitor.

---

* The essentials of justification were illustrated and explained, for the first time as far as I know, by Walter Tracy in *Letters of credit* (London: Gordon Fraser, 1986).

16 Sequence of design and production

Anyone with a fair amount of experience in writing, drawing and designing letters knows when the forms and the whole concept are properly defined on paper – or even just in your own mind. You know that the next step is production. Production starts with the so-called control characters. These are the characters composed of the parts or elements that recur frequently in other characters of the whole design. In lowercase roman, the control characters are often n and o; with the capitals, control characters are H and O. These characters are brought into balance with each other, in their height, weight, and width. When this has been done, other characters can be derived, by comparing and fitting them to the control characters. It is quite useless to start with, say, an s and go on to a t. The essential necessity for good visual co-operation between height, weight, and width – in short, for balance and harmony – demands a certain order of production. Neglecting this order is like shooting randomly in the air, hoping that one day a duck might fall down.

This order is no different for us than it was for Granjon and his contemporaries. Balance doesn't come free. To achieve it, you must have a keen eye for visual values, and a strict order of working. If now we start by accurately designing the n and the o, so too the punchcutter first made the counters of n and o. He brought the shapes of the counters into balance with each other, before knowing the final forms of the n and o. We see a character as a whole form, whereas the punchcutter divided it into two constituent parts: the inner and the outer. This conception followed from – or interacted with – the technique of punchcutting. And it happened also that this conception resulted in a better understanding of the principles of visual balance. I would say it was this, together with working at true size, that gave us products which are still unbeaten in visual quality, and still the basis for much present-day text type.

17 One punch a day?

Nothing is as undervalued and unregarded as time. How much time did a sixteenth-century punchcutter need to cut a font? The usually accepted average rate of work is one punch a day. But this can be doubted, certainly for easy punches such as the point, comma, brackets, and so forth. With these characters one can easily make up to three or four punches a day. The figures I give here are based on my own experience.

Some of the work could be given to a goldsmith or to a pupil. He would be engaged to make little pieces of steel of the right length, not too thick and not too thin, and well annealed too. The punchcutter now hit the required counter shape into the steel with an already existing counterpunch. That might take around fifteen minutes. The next day, the punchcutter would bring it to the right height: thirty minutes. All the superfluous material was filed away: thirty minutes. So to make one punch to just the right height has taken the punchcutter about one and a quarter hours.

Now comes the more delicate work: the fine tuning of the shape, with the means of very fine files and gravers. For a lowercase l this is obviously much less work than for a lowercase a. But it would not have been more than two hours per punch. We have now clocked up three and a quarter hours for the average punch. For three punches that is nine and three-quarter hours. People did not observe eight-hour working days then. So, in summer, a punchcutter could easily manage four punches a day. Accepting that there are 120 punches in a font: that means thirty days. And even if we suppose that I am out by a half, then it comes to two months for a complete font.

There is another factor here, more difficult to discuss, which must have affected time of production. This is the quality of steel. Experienced modern punchcutters do not like to work with twentieth-century industrial steel. Proper steel for cutting punches by hand is hard to find nowadays. I have said that 'steel can be like butter'. But if I accept what some experienced men have told me, then steel can be even more like butter than I know.

18 Where are the counterpunches?

Although not the final product, punches are of great interest to type historians. Scarcer and less regarded than punches are counterpunches. That every sixteenth-century punchcutter used counterpunches is, I have argued in chapter 14, beyond doubt. Nevertheless hardly any counterpunches of real value have survived. In the Plantin-Moretus Museum there are about 4,500 punches – and just 16 counterpunches.

I have suggested (chapter 11) that if a punchcutter had a well-balanced set of counterpunches, then half the job of cutting punches was done. They must have been very important to the punchcutter. If he sold a set of punches, it would be possible, with the counterpunches, to make a new design of the same quality. Thus a punchcutter could quickly copy his own work. Besides this, counterpunches were a good point of reference for cutting larger and also smaller sizes of a design. Say I want to make a small pica font, having already made a font in the slightly smaller long primer size: then it is very handy to be able to compare the necessary counterpunches. They will not differ much from each other. Comparing counterpunches of neighbouring sizes, you soon understand that they belong to the same typeface. Sometimes it is possible to make different fonts of a typeface with one set of counterpunches. Of course, now and then you have to adjust a little.

The great men of the sixteenth century, to whom we have referred so often, clearly had astonishing outputs. This was possible not merely through their use of counterpunches from character to character in one font. They would also have made characters in several sizes with the help of one set of counterpunches [18.1]. On top of this, I think that their counterpunches gradually changed with use – like a pencil growing smaller and smaller – and that maybe they even passed from master to pupil. The very first types of Garamond could well have been done with the help of counterpunches (slightly adapted or maybe even unchanged) made by his master Antoine Augereau.

The huge quantity of type – it can hardly be called anything else – that Nicolas Kis cut can be explained by extensive reuse of counterpunches over more than one design, and perhaps by the help of an assistant. And also by the probable fact that he either bought or otherwise acquired counterpunches from Dirk Voskens.

The men who bought punches were other punchcutters or printers. When buying material from the heirs of a recently deceased colleague, a punchcutter would certainly have known the value of a complete set of counterpunches. Printers did not realize the importance of them, however, and counterpunches were not included in the sales of their property. At least there is no record of this; and certainly our museums give them no attention, even if they possess them. But if I were a sixteenth-century punchcutter, I would certainly not sell my counterpunches, for all the reasons given here. If Plantin, for example, had realized the importance of counterpunches, he would have bought them together with the punches he acquired: as a quick and efficient means of making replacements for any punches that got broken. Counterpunches coming into the possession of people who did not cut punches would have languished, not understood. Eventually they would have been discarded or treated as scrap metal.

18.1

A counterpunch could be used to make the counters for more than one size of type.

19 Hendrik van den Keere and outlines

If the French punchcutters dominated the scene in the sixteenth century, Hendrik van den Keere was one of the few North-European punchcutters whom one can consider in the same breath. He is their equal in output, in skill, and style too.

Van den Keere was a true counterpunch man, even more so than his colleagues. His punches show us that he used counterpunches whenever possible: the sides of his counters tend to be steeper than those of his contemporaries. Roman text typefaces were his staple work, of course; but he also cut blackletter and music type. His oeuvre contains some highly unusual pieces: large display letters. By 'large' I mean sizes beyond the reach of the punchcutter. Naturally the size of these letters had consequences for the technique of producing them. The 'punches' for these letters were of wood, and these punches were pressed into 'matrices' of sand, from which metal type was cast. So, instead of cutting in metal, Van den Keere had to engrave in wood, following a contour. Then he dug out the shapes described by the engraved line. How did he make the outline? By drawing. And this brings him closer to us.

To start designing a letter by drawing has serious disadvantages, compared with Van den Keere's usual way of working – punchcutting. The character has to be drawn all in one go, instead of first just the counters, as is the case with cutting text sizes in metal. Another disadvantage: drawing here means the making of a contour or outline. A contour does not present a form. A contour only describes the border or edge of a certain form. Compare it with a thin sheet of glass in which you cut out a letter. You do not see the letter, because it is made of glass. You look right through it. The only thing you see is the border, where the glass ends. And a third disadvantage of drawing – which must sound strange to anyone who has not worked at true size – is the relatively large scale of work.

These are disadvantages that punchcutting avoids, and they could be the reasons for the typical beginner's mistakes that Van den Keere made with these display letters [19. 1]. He certainly wasn't inexperienced. Six years before this he had made his two-line Double Pica: a roman with an x-height of about 7 mm, and of course entirely cut in metal [19.2]. This 7 mm is half of the x-height we are discussing here. The Double Pica roman is a good design with a clear unity. So Van den Keere's own work should have provided a reference point, and, although large romans were still rare, he might have known the type used in some books printed in Lyons by Jean de Tournes. Around 1550 this printer used a very elegant large roman of comparable x-height that, on stylistic grounds, can be attributed to Granjon.* If Granjon was indeed responsible for that type, then there is a good chance that Van den Keere knew about it. Yet the 'plus grande romaine' shows us a beginner's mistakes in all their glory. Many strokes are too thin or too thick. Some counters are too big or too small. The whole design, however, shows a typeface with a strong character. This is no accident. Like any experienced punchcutter, Van den Keere had strong ideas about what a roman typeface should look like. In the 'plus grande romaine', this strong sense, rooted in punchcutting experience, comes up against his lack of experience in designing with outlines.

* This is reproduced in Jan Tschichold's *Treasury of alphabets and lettering* (New York: Reinhold, 1966, p. 126). Tschichold's suggestion for the punchcutter was Guillaume Le Bé I.

19.1
(overleaf) Hendrik van den Keere was an experienced punchcutter when he produced this type, yet the design shows beginner's mistakes. From our point of view the thick/thin contrast is extreme, although this was a tendency of its time. The variations in stem width suggest that this is a first attempt. Notice also the lowercase v (too wide), and the angles of the counters of the o's (with and without accents) which differ noticeably. (Van den Keere's 7-line roman, earliest appearance 1576, reproduced same size.)

abcde

fghijlm

nopqrſs

tuvyz

x&œ

ā ē ñ ō p̄ ū

ff ffi ffi ffl ffl fi

fi ſſ ſſi ſſi ſt

þ̣ ꝑ̣ ꝑ ı ꝙ ꝰ ꝓ

(â : ô - û ?

Typographic historians have often puzzled over this design, and wondered about its surprising clumsiness. Speculations of all kinds have been made: for example, that Van den Keere did not cut the design himself. But if somebody else cut it, then it would have been much easier for him to reject it. So he probably did cut it himself, but was perhaps confused by the large size, the unfamiliar technique of cutting in wood, and his attempt to condense certain counters (h, n, m, u) as much as possible towards proportions that would be more suitable for textura. Uncertainty piled on uncertainty. In the end he may just have shrugged his shoulders and let it pass. By contrast, in the case of his large textura type there would have been plentiful examples around him: on painted signs, tombstones, stained glass.

So Van den Keere made a mistake. While embarking on a new technique of drawing letters on wood, he relied too much on his knowledge of forms made with another technique. He was too confident to stop and think clearly about it. Or perhaps he was too lazy – say, to paint the surface of the wood black, and then cut the letters out, seeing clearly what he was taking away.

19.2
Two of Van den Keere's punches for his two-line Double Pica roman.

This example lets us think further about drawing for punchcut typefaces. No drawings or sketches survive for typefaces cut in the sixteenth century. If precise drawings had been made, they would have been things of value – even just in terms of the time spent in making them – and so have a chance of survival. But I doubt very much whether any were ever made. Speaking from my own experience, it is not necessary to draw neatly before cutting. The only kind of drawing I can imagine being made is a quick and loose sketch: not a working drawing. If such sketches were indeed made, they would have been attempts at the mood or feeling of the letters. If punchcutters at that time had been used to making neat working drawings, then this typeface of Van den Keere's would not have been so clumsy. Drawing out letters at large sizes was certainly not unknown then: look at the precisely measured alphabets of Dürer and Tory, or at the alphabets in the books of the writing masters. But no punchcutter of the time attempted a formal explanation of his work, least of all by means of large drawn letters.

20 Linearity

The idea of linear fonts is interesting. It has been raised, lost, and raised again, as the techniques of type production have changed over the centuries. 'Linearity' means the simple enlargement and reduction from a single 'master' font.

We tend to think that, in the sixteenth century, different sizes of type constituted different designs. With the italics cut by Granjon, this is no doubt true. He loved to experiment and he seems to make variations with each new size. But in fact the idea of fonts with a linear progression is much older than we think. It is not as old as typography itself, but the difference is not more than a hundred years.

We only need to look at the strong and efficient romans of Pierre Haultin to realize that they share a marked family resemblance. In chapter 18, I speculated that counterpunches were used for more than one size of a design, and this technical fact may have played a part in producing common features. But I can't help thinking that Haultin cut his romans with a single, recurring model in his mind. They show peculiar details that return in every size; and there is purpose in their return. This suggests strongly that Haultin thought about designing type in a linear way. Of course his types are not completely linear, and they certainly do not show the visual shortcomings of true linear fonts. Such a thing is not possible when the human eye is in sole control, as was the case in Haultin's time. But his fonts are as linear as one could get in those days. If you take a close look at his work, it is clear that Haultin could never have thought along the lines of 'last spring I made size 9, this summer I need size 12 too – now what should it look like?'

The following illustrations show four romans attributed to Pierre Haultin in use (reproduced same size). Exactly when each was cut, we do not know, but they were probably cut over a period of about 10 years, c. 1550–60. Haultin strived for no-nonsense efficiency and logic. A number of peculiarities recur in his types. For example, his capital R's always have rather cramped tails, probably for better fitting. His italic capitals are strange and faulty: but faulty with reason and consistency. His typical lowercase a is a bit askew. His rather open lowercase g is generous both in the closed upper counter and in the open lower one. These are two further peculiarities that can be seen enlarged in illustrations 20.5–20.8.

20.1
*(p. 138) Nonpareille Romaine (c. 6 pt). 'Probably the first type for so small a body, used frequently by Plantin from 1557 on.' (*Libri regum ..., *Antwerp: Plantin, 1557.)*

20.2
(p. 139) Coronelle Romaine (c. 7 pt. 'A fine little letter much used by Plantin from 1566 until 1573, after which it is gradually replaced by Van den Keere's Coronel.' (P. A. Toparius, Conciones ..., *Antwerp: Plantin, 1567.)*

20.3
(p. 140) Philosophie Romaine (c. 10 pt). 'A handsome face, used frequently by Plantin from 1561 until he acquired Van den Keere's Philosophie in 1579.' (G. Rondeletius, De ponderibus ..., *Antwerp: Plantin, 1561.)*

20.4
(p. 141) Augustine Romaine (c. 14 pt). 'A handsome face of interesting proportions, used occasionally by Plantin from 1561.' (Raevardus, Tribonianus, *Antwerp: Plantin, 1561.)*

Quotations are taken from the Inventory of the Plantin-Moretus Museum.

non vt consolarentur Hanon, dixerũt prin-
cipes filiorum Ammon ad Hanon, Tu forsitan
putas, quòd Dauid honoris causa in patrem
tuum misericqui consolarentur te : nec ani,
maduertis, quòd vt explorent, & inuestigent,
& scrutentur terram tuã venerint ad te ser-
ui eius. Igitur Hanon pueros Dauid decal-
uauit & rasit & præcidit tunicas eorum à
natibus vsque ad pedes, & dimisit eos. Qui
cùm abiissent, & hoc mãdassent Dauid, misit
in occursum eorum (grandem enim contu-
meliam sustinuerant) & præcepit vt manerét
in Iericho, donec cresceret barba eorum, &
tunc reuerterentur. Videntes autem filii
Ammon, quòd iniuriam fecissent Dauid tam
Hanon quàm reliquus populus, miserũt mil-
le talenta argenti, vt conducerent sibi de Me-
sopotamia, & de Syria Maacha, & de Soba
currus & equites. Conduxeruntque trigin-
ta duo millia curruum, & regem Maacha cũ
populo eius. Qui cùm venissent, castrametati
sunt è regione Medaba. Filii quoque Ammon
congregati de vrbibus suis, venerunt ad bellum. Quod cùm audisset Dauid, misit Ioab
& omnem exercitum virorum fortium :
egressíque filii Ammon, direxerunt aciem
iuxta portam ciuitatis : reges autem qui ad
auxilium eius venerant, separatim in agro
steterunt. Igitur Ioab intelligens bellum ex
aduerso, & post tergum contra se fieri, elegit
viros fortissimos de vniuerso Israel, & perrexit contra Syrum. Reliquam autem partem
populi dedit sub manu Abisai fratris sui : &
perrexerunt contra filios Ammon. Dixítq́;,
Si vicerit me Syrus, auxilio eris mihi : Si autem superauerint te filii Ammon, ero tibi in
præsidium. Confortare, & agamus viriliter
pro populo nostro, & pro vrbibus Dei nostri:
Dominus autem quod in conspectu suo bo-
num est, faciet. Perrexit ergo Ioab, & populus qui cum eo erat, contra Syrum ad præ-

s   lium

INDEX

quuti. Nam, quã me olim R O N D E L E T I V S
docuit, fcriptóq; tradidit morborum dignofcen-
dorum & curandorũ regulam, religiofiſsimè ob-
feruás, iam ferè feptennium Medicinam exerceo.
Vnde præter haud vulgarem famam fauſtis & fæ-
pe inopinatis fuccefsibus partam, amicorum in
multis regionibus iuſtum numerũ (vt interim de
lucro, quod Medicum nõ decet, nihil dicam) mihi
comparaui. Noſtri ergo æmulatione accenfi, ò iu-
uenes, R O N D E L E T I I certiſsimam facilli-
mámq; methodum amplectimini: ab ea ne latum
quidem vnguê (quod aiunt) difcedite: R O N D E-
L E T I I non libros, fed thefauros auidius expe-
tite, conceſſos memoriæ fcriniolis fecretioribus
includite, vt cùm erit opus, reclufos in humani
generis falutem fœliciter difpenfetis. Hunc, quem
in lucê prodire finit, alij multi (vt fperamus) bre-
ui comitabuntur, quorum nobis iamdudum co-
piam fecit, & per quos plurimum ἐν ἰἀϑρικῇ profe-
ciſſe fatemur. Non equidem inuideo, nec de præ-
ceptore conqueror: vt ferunt Alexandrum regem
ægrè tuliſſe : quòd difciplinas ἀκροαμαλικὰς libris
foras editis inuulgaſſet Ariſtoteles, quibus ab eo
ipfe eruditus foret. Quin R O N D E L E T I V M
hortor, vt quod fe, id eſt magnificum in re Medi-
ca imperatorê decet, omnibus Medicinæ ſtudio-
fis vel amplius quàm nobis, fi fieri poſsit, bene fa-
ciat, & futuro quoque æuo profpiciat, neque id
tam immortalitatis ſtudio (etfi digniſsimo virtutis
aculeo) quàm liberalitatis & candoris nomine,
quibus hic totus effulget . Nam fibi fatis gloriæ
iam quæfiuit, poſſetque definere, ni animᵒ inquies
pafceretur ijs operibus quæ humano generi pro-
futura videt, quæque fuis laudem maximam ad-
ferre poſſe nouit. Hunc ergo numinis inſtar coli-
te, φιλιαλροι, qui Medicinam facturi ducem quæ-
ritis : huius theoremata præceptionéfque , velut
ab ora-

tur,cap.xxvij.de pact. & hæc quidem fic
olim erant in vfu āte Scriboniam legem.

L A T A deinde lege Scribonia ciuilis 5
hæc feruitutum vfucapio penitus exole-
uit:& quæ antea ciuili iure duorum an-
norum fpatio acquirebantur feruitutes,
ftatim poft Scriboniam legem ex edicto
prætoris acquiri longo tempore cœpe-
runt.Scribit enim Aggenus Vrbicus in
Frontinum, biennio iter quod in vfu e-
rat vfucapi potuiffe. Iter, inquit, nō qua ,,
ad culturas peruenitur,capitur vfu,fed id ,,
quod in vfu biennio fuit. Quinque enim ,,
aut fex pedum latitudinem in agrorum
finibus conftituit lex Mamilia: eámque
iter ad culturas accedens fic occupabat,
vt vfucapi non poffet.Iter igitur quà ad
culturas peruenitur, hoc eft commune il
lud iter quod ex lege Mamilia aliquam
itineris publici naturam induerat,vfu re-
liquarum rerum publicarum exéplo non
acquirebatur : fed quod in vfu biennio
fuit,hoc eft,fed illud iter recte capieba-
tur vfu, quo quis priuato quodā & pro-
prio feruitutis iure vfus erat biennio . Vt
ita quidem feruitutes ante Scriboniam legem biennio vfu captas fuiffe non
                                   fit du-

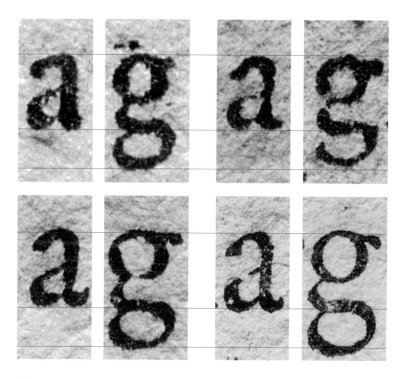

20.5
Nonpareille Romaine,
enlarged 20 times.

20.6
Coronelle Romaine,
enlarged 17 times.

20.7
Philosophie Romaine,
enlarged 12 times.

20.8
Augustine Romaine,
enlarged 9 times.

*Letters from the types shown in illustrations 20.1–20.4, enlarged to the same
x-height. They show a strong resemblance to each other, and confirm that Haultin
had a strong, fixed idea of what a roman should look like. Another interesting
point suggested here: we tend to assume that a typeface for a small body needs to
be wider than one for a larger body. Haultin does not follow this rule. Instead he
justified small characters rather widely, and this gives the eye the scanning time
it needs for reading text at small sizes.*

Punchcutting and the working of type

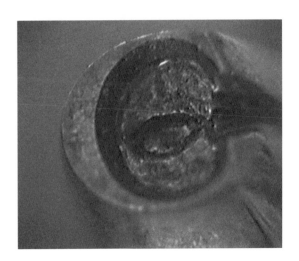

*This punch for capital C is by Granjon. It clearly shows what Fournier suggests
in his discussion of cutting punches for larger type (*Manuel typographique,
*chapter 4). 'After a slight impression has been made on the punch, the hollow
is drilled with a twist-drill, then with little hard-tempered cold chisels and a
hammer the corners or unwanted metal inside of the letter are chipped away and
the counterpunch is put in the hole and struck in with a hammer until it leaves its
impression.' The little hole that we see in the middle of the bottom of the counter
is a left-over from the first hole, made in the way that Fournier describes.*

144

21 Does technique influence form?

Every way of working leaves its characteristic marks and shapes, which have their advantages and disadvantages. The material itself will invite the punchcutter to do some things and not others. We have seen that the punchcutter can work very accurately: right to the limits of human visual perception. In theory, but not in practice, the punchcutter meets no technical or material obstacles. In practice, through certain habits or ways of working, some typical and recurrent shapes result. Having acknowledged that, we can still say that a punchcutter can make what he wants. To show this, it is enough to refer to the astonishing example of the first civilité punches.

Looking closely at the punches for civilité type, as well as at the printed characters, it occurs to me that their makers understood more about letterforms than we do today. We tend to stick to our rather formal romans and italics: simple shapes in comparison with most civilité letters. An expert punchcutter in the middle of the sixteenth century had to deal with a wide range of scripts: not just roman and its italic companion, but broken scripts like textura and civilité; Greek and Hebrew were common, and there was music type too. By the end of the sixteenth century there was a growing demand for Arabic type. All of these scripts and notations present different problems. For example, civilité is quite different from roman [3.7]. This difference is not just a matter of its delicate, complex, curly forms. The disposition of the letters is lying down, rather than – as in roman – standing up. Further, civilité demands a greater freedom of rhythm, while achieving good, balanced word-images too. So, it presents different design problems.

The idea that there are no obstacles in punchcutting can be qualified as follows. Take two lowercase n's [21.1]. The way the process goes – its 'grain', perhaps – means that the second n is easier and more obvious as a form than the first n. This follows from the nature of the cutting tool. Any instrument has its own obvious process of

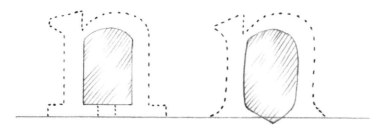

21.1

The aesthetic qualities of the first n are those of simple rationality.
Everything is neat and straight. This is the ideal.
The second n is certainly an n, but not informed by any simple rationality.

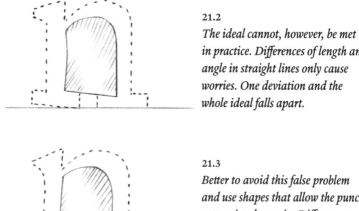

21.2

The ideal cannot, however, be met in practice. Differences of length and angle in straight lines only cause worries. One deviation and the whole ideal falls apart.

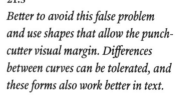

21.3

Better to avoid this false problem and use shapes that allow the punch-cutter visual margin. Differences between curves can be tolerated, and these forms also work better in text.

use. The nature of a brush, for example, is such that you are invited to pull and not to push it. Not only do the tools invite the punchcutter to make the second n, but also this shape is easier to handle in the rest of the process of type design and punchcutting. It has no straight lines and no sharp corners. And the absence of these hard elements makes the form of the second n more acceptable to the human eye than that of the first. This more subtle shape has notable visual margin or tolerance. Hard straight lines make us wonder whether they really are straight or not [21.2]. If they are indeed not quite straight, this is awkward to look at. So the punchcutter avoided such niggling questions and situations by building in a kind of visual doubt: no straight edges, no sharp corners [21.3]. The forms become easy to handle, easy to mix and to bring into balance with each other.

We must not forget that the punchcutter worked at the real or final size of the type and that first he only made the counterpunches for the most important characters. This means, for example, that if he made a counter for 10 point type, this would be about 0.5 or 1 mm in width. Or it means that the eye of the lowercase 'e' would be about 0.2 to 0.3 mm in width: smaller than the thickness of a bristle on your toothbrush. This is quite different from the way we work today. Now, on a screen, we are able to see letterforms as big as our hands. One might think that a punchcutter's magnifying glass removes this difference. But the work itself – the cutting of the punch – is still done at the final, true size. On our present-day screens we can enlarge the image not just to get a better look, but also to enhance the accuracy of control over possible changes. That kind of measured accuracy is not possible at true size. My guess is that punchcutters would push themselves into a position where they did not quite know what they were changing. They just had to look at the result and see if they liked it. They began, with experience, to rely increasingly on intuition. I can't help feeling that this must have been an exciting way to work.

Another point to remember is the frame of reference. The punchcutter had no reference points: no baseline and no vertical axis either. When was something really straight or upright? A punchcutter would never know. But it was probably not seen as a real problem: he knew that to strive for mathematical perfection was a hopeless search. He also knew that if he tried to take out the imperfections this would lead to an endless journey of correction and insecurity. No, the punch-cutters were not stupid, but knew that these charming imperfections were necessary and that they gave room to play: a margin where the experienced eye could work fast, in ease and comfort.

People like a certain comfort. This wish for ease is always very important in production. Type design for a punchcutter includes many manual activities: not just punchcutting but justifying matrices as well; although casting type was done – at maximum speed – by other people. Looking at their output, it is clear that these early punch-cutters were producers as well as designers. So ease in making and producing must have been important for them. The punchcutters of this period seem to command a very fine mixture of efficiency and aesthetics. For these men, punches and justified matrices were the products that earned their daily bread. For them, more than for some printers, type was essentially a means of producing commercial and efficient books. Commerce was as important as aesthetics. Yet it was certainly important to them to produce type of high aesthetic or visual quality.

One wonders about these matters on finding, in one set of punches, three lowercase a's, two m's, and three e's. These were not made because the a punch would break sooner or more easily than the i, for example. No, the answer to this question can only be that the punchcutters enjoyed cutting punches. They must have had much pleasure in making an m or a g: so much so that they made a few of them, and then simply could not decide which one was best. Total control over the material and high technical skill provide true freedom. It is this that enables the real master not to live by the rules but to absorb and then transcend them. This is independent of technique. In this respect there is no difference between a sixteenth-century punchcutter and somebody from the digital era who draws a letter on a computer screen. But a punchcutter cannot make a back-up.

148

21.4
*This manuscript from Northern France (c. 1300) shows the freedom enjoyed
by an experienced scribe. There is a constant adjustment in the forms of characters,
to enable better fit. (Enlarged to 150%.)*

149

Now one can raise some questions about the little optical adjustments that a punchcutter left in his work. This visual fiddling seems a bit doubtful to the design rationality of our age. You might say that the punchcutter avoided mathematical truth and therefore avoided problems that might cause him to doubt. But I think they were right to do it like that. There was no other way. Their whole world would have educated them to think like this: or certainly that part of the world that consists of letters. Scribes constantly and instinctively do the same. In manuscripts, every single letter is manipulated to let it fit well into its surroundings [21.4]. It is a strange phenomenon and one that happens at the moment of creation. But if you look closely you see that written letters always stand askew. Optical balance is constantly created and corrected; for example, by making one serif longer than another, or by leaving it off the letter when circumstances require that.

The punchcutter does all these things with his smoke-proofs, but much more slowly. Like the scribe, he looks at a letter in its true size and comes to judgements based on the balance of the letter itself and on its balance in relation to the other letters. The punchcutter has of course to consider things much more carefully than a scribe does: he is making a set of signs that have to be combined with each other in a huge number of permutations. But he cannot see the results in text, and has to rely on a backlog of experience. Present-day designers have a great advantage here: we can check letters in text, as a punchcutter could not. However experienced, the punchcutter could not and did not stop to consider too long.

With present techniques we can define the slightest change very accurately. This is something that a punchcutter was not bothered with. He only worked on things he could see: if he did not see it, then it did not exist. I think this is an advantage that has been lost for ever. We are even afraid to rely on our own nervous system. Instead we have to be convinced by numbers (co-ordinates) rather than by visual evidence. Even experienced type designers get confused when they have to check the justification of an old design. The design looks good,

but the numbers look bad. The consequence is too much dead type.
We think that if we make the numbers correct then the result must be
good. Even if some designers like to work in this way, human beings
certainly do not read like this. I try to explain why in the next chapter.

Today's techniques are certainly leaving their marks on type
design and even on the use of type. Designers may make things for no
reason other than that technique allows it. And so, in Western thinking, it seems logical to do it. But technique is there for us and not the
other way around. For example, designers who use 4 point type in
serious reading matter do not know what they are doing. The fact that
technique can easily reproduce 4 point type is no excuse. In the same
way, rational and technical typefaces might look well-designed for
present-day purposes, certainly when you look at them in large sizes.
And they are indeed good designs, as long as you use them big. But
do not compose a book in such a typeface: after a few pages you will
be disappointed.

22 The unconscious eye

Technical developments have made it possible to work very precisely in drawing letters. The fact of precision gives us the sense that we have done a job correctly too. It is a comfortable feeling. This digital precision lies beyond human perception. It is just as with hi-fi audio equipment, where even experts cannot hear difference in sound quality, but need instruments to measure it. Then they can say that installation X is, by a certain percentage, better than installation Y. So with type. Often typographers do not look at what is in front of them, but rather they judge it by using technical knowledge that lurks at the back of their minds. This is not a good way to proceed.

Most typefaces – certainly any belonging to the Garamond category – should have optical irregularity and variety if they are to function satisfactorily. This is not a shortcoming of the punchcutter or of punchcutting technique. Rather, it is a positive quality, and one that has been lost. Whether the early punchcutters really understood this, is, in the end, not open to us to know. What is interesting and relevant for us is the question of whether we can bring 'imperfection' back under present conditions of design and production. With steel and gravers the punchcutter also had a high-precision instrument. But he depended on its precision only when that was useful. The limits of precision are determined by human factors: by the limits of human perception. By working in that way, the types of the old masters often gained a quality that can hardly be found today. This quality cannot be explained merely by imperfect printing techniques. Rather, it has to do with all the imperfections and irregularities that balance on the border of what can be perceived.

Three factors that make for variety in text can be distinguished. First, irregularity in the border between the black of a character and the white of the paper. Secondly, the fact of real differences in the shape of the same character at different occurrences. Thirdly, unevenness in the surface of the paper. You can see this clearly in the contrast between a 300 dpi laser-printed page – where all these factors are present – and the same text output by an image-setter onto photographic paper – where they are all absent.

Reading is a process of scanning an awful lot of monotonous information that obviously means something. Our eyes and brain have to be trained to carry out this task; it is not a natural one. A page composed in hair-sharp type, designed by an over-rational mind, will tend to look like a pebble beach made up of just one pebble, repeated millions of times. Or like a tree with leaves of only one form, or a meadow with blades of grass of exactly the same height, colour, thickness, and

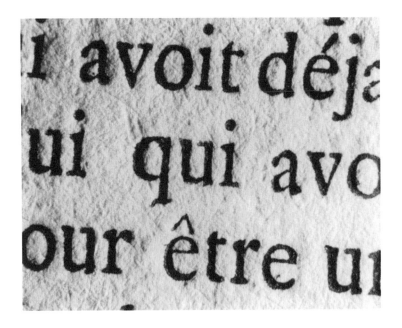

22.1

The photograph may be a little dramatized in its effects, but it shows clearly the qualities of hand-production in type, paper, and printing. We see attractive variations in weight of the characters, in the letterforms themselves, in depth of impression, and there is a soft border between areas of absolute black and absolute white: values that are hard to achieve now. (Printed 1715.)

direction. The reader's brain will be very confused. It does not know where to look. In dealing with a large monotonous quantity of something, it needs random imperfections.

Let me try another explanation of reading – one based just on reflections on my own experience. Although I cannot possibly prove any of this, some such account is needed to make sense of these things. So: there are two levels of seeing. By 'seeing' I do not mean just how the eyes work, which is something that one can find out from books easily enough. But rather I mean 'how the brain processes what is perceived': something that isn't so easy to find clear answers to.

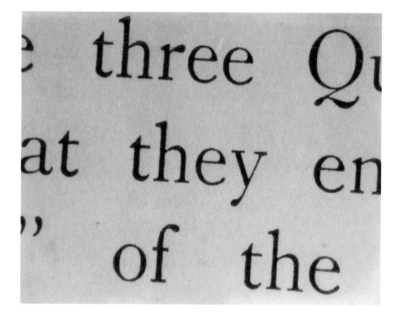

22.2
Letterforms with high contrast between thick and thin strokes, extremely smooth paper, a razor-sharp border between black and white. By the end of the nineteenth century, printers thought that this perfection improved on the bad craftsmanship of hand-production. (Printed 1908.)

There is actual, conscious seeing. And there is a more or less unconscious level of seeing. They occur simultaneously.

We see much that we are not aware of. Take a simple example. You are walking in the countryside, focusing sharply at a point in the distance. Suddenly to one side of you, a bird flies off. You see it out of the corner of your eye, although you were not looking at it, but rather at some point 200 metres in front of you. Yet the part of the brain that looks after unconscious seeing makes you look at the bird, maybe as a protection against possible danger. As a pedestrian in a city, you do not mind the cars that drive fast along the road: you grow used to

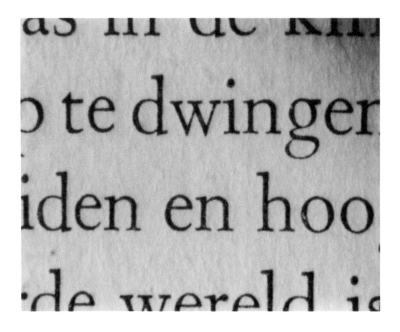

22.3
The qualities of the hand-made page are evident here, in this piece of industrial production: Monotype composition, printed letterpress on appropriate paper. The result is well-balanced and acceptable. (Printed 1951.)

neglecting them. There is a part of you that registers all this, but not at a conscious level.

Unconscious seeing must communicate or co-operate strongly with conscious seeing. So, in what we call reflex action, you find your-self doing things that you had no intention of doing. Unconscious seeing covers the whole area of seeing outside the area of sharp focus. It is difficult to control, but at some level it can be done. Unconscious seeing has to be controlled in reading, especially when you are learn-ing to read. Then it has to accept this very particular state of affairs – state of mind – of looking only 40 centimetres into the distance and

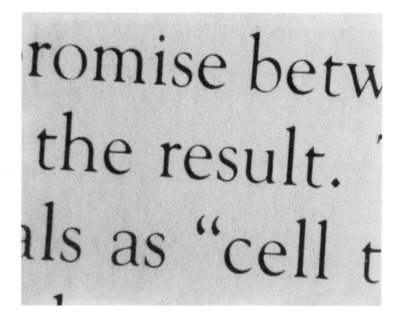

22.4
Digital photoset type, printed by offset lithography. The typeface is designed as just a single master outline: characters are too thin and so too brilliant. Paper is smooth and white, and there is a sharp border between black and white. (Printed 1988.)

avoiding the rest of the scene. When this state is achieved, the conscious part of the brain has sufficient energy available for it to take on the process of recognizing and processing words. The balance between conscious and unconscious remains in play, even after the technique of reading has been learned. Thus, you may be an experienced reader, able to concentrate deeply, and reading a text of great interest, when out of the blue, your unconscious sight springs into action: 'look there, a fly walking along the top of the page!' You can't not see such things.

Typography has to take care of this unconscious seeing: not by building fly-fences, but by removing the factors that set off alarms and so interfere with reading. Yet also, I think that unconscious seeing starts to ring alarms when it is given nothing to do. This would be a way to explain what happens with text on very white and very smooth paper, and set in characters that have an absolute border – so that there is an abrupt change from 100 per cent black to 100 per cent white. A character that is exactly the same at each occurrence can lead to confusion too, if not to boredom. And tiny marks that need energy to detect: are they there or not? All these things in combination mean that the unconscious eye does not know where to look. It wants to find something to hold on to. You get the feeling of not being able to keep your eyes on the page. The unconscious part goes on strike and stops co-operating with the conscious part. You lift your eyes from the page, and look at something else. Then the unconscious eye is released. You think your eyes itch. Or you assume that you are tired, because the same thing happens when your body is actually tired. But you were just torturing yourself with a page of text.

To the future

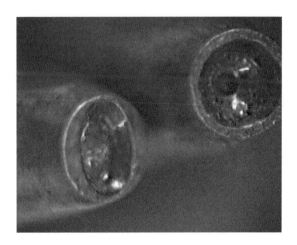

Two punches from a set made by Granjon. Left is the lowercase o, while on the right we see the zero. The bottoms of the two counters are quite different from each other. It looks as if Granjon must have thought 'well, a zero is perfectly round, so I might as well just drill that counter': and in his day it was customary to represent the zero with a perfectly round form. Both punches are attributed to Granjon on grounds of their finishing.

23 Punchcutting in the digital age

Printing has always been a rather closed business. The early printers kept their knowledge to themselves. Eventually the typographer or typographic designer emerged, as someone who could control the process of print production, and mediate with people outside. Then around the middle of the twentieth century, the person we call the graphic designer began to be identified. Among their other differences from typographers, graphic designers had a closer relationship with the ordinary life of societies. They reached out beyond book typography, to design any item of printing or communication, including many not previously dreamed of. The so-called democratization of typography began to occur in the 1950s and 1960s, when typewriters, transfer lettering, small-offset printing presses, and photocopiers became available for use by lay people. Now personal computers and laser printers have taken this process much further. A certain degree of typographic consciousness has become more common in non-specialist people, and the potential is there for a much wider spread of knowledge and awareness. The traditional gentleman-typographers, and the type designers who depend on them, have been pushed out of their studies. Or, if they have not yet been pushed, the closed and untroubled atmosphere in which they have surrounded themselves becomes less and less plausible.

We used to say 'printing type' or 'printers type', but this term has lost its meaning. Printers are now just people who run printing presses: type is used by other kinds of people. And anyway, its use on paper becomes less significant, now that we find type moving around on screens, on buildings, and in every other medium. Knowledge has been spread by the printed word. But this knowledge has brought us to where we are now: still very much dependent on the printed word, but also having to deal with a much more open and complicated set of circumstances.

Here we can stop and ask what this book, and the subject of

punchcutting, has to offer to anyone grappling with these present conditions of design and information transfer. The answer could be: next to nothing. Designers, students, even teachers, do not need to know about how metal type was made. They can do their work without this knowledge. But that will then happen at the minimum level of brutal function and basic economics. Although even at that level it may help to be able to answer questions such as 'why does old type look so shaky?', and 'I want a blurry typeface, why has this blurriness gone from type?'

A book like this one finds its place at a higher level: at the level of the question 'what is the value of history?' But that apparently abstract question also belongs to daily necessity. Because without such knowledge you float, without direction. History is there anyway, and it helps to know about it. In the long haul of human history, as in the short haul of our individual lives, discovering or remembering what happened in the early days can be essential for life in the present. This isn't to say that there is a ready-made history there to be discovered. History changes constantly. New discoveries, new perspectives constantly change the shape of what is known. Facts, data, and the knowledge of them, is not what I mean by history. Rather, history is more like a puzzle that we try to complete, but which will always be unfinished. We look for patterns that make sense.

But why? What for? To let you – you the reader – compare now with then. In the colleges and universities, history is sometimes just the material of academic careers. But history is a human right and should be open to everyone. It is the way in which we represent ourselves, think and feel about ourselves, in which we create our cultures. History is not primarily a story about 'where we come from', about heritage or ancestry. It is more immediate than that. What history can do is help us to feel connected with the things that we do and are interested in. Forget the school history of great men and great events. For every imaginable subject or activity there is a history to be constructed. Do not believe that it need only be about high culture in the arts, sciences, politics, religion, and wars. Do not accept that it is limited by what can be read on paper in archives. It needs much less paperwork than the professional historians like to admit. It is quite possible that a young rock guitarist, reflecting on his own way of solving musical problems, can say much more interesting things about Paganini than a biographer who knows all the facts of the great musician's life. History needs to become much more active, and so it needs to abandon its academic inhibitions. In principle, history hardly has rules, fixed angles or methods. It is all about reconsidering what we know, looking at what has been newly discovered or rethought. It is a procedure of constant revaluation.

The history of typography is hard to get hold of, incomplete, unclear, wrong, just too old, or perhaps not old enough. You have to work for it. Maybe this book can help here. At least now it is clear to me that sitting and looking at punches is not enough. If you want to understand these things, then you have to make some yourself. I recommend to the theoreticians that they have a go at making some of these things of which they speak so knowledgeably.

For example, it is interesting to discover how much was done already in the first 150 years of printing. Among these discoveries, one thinks first of the break with the limits implied in writing: in size of letter and line increment. There was the birth of an overall awareness of typographic processes, including development of standard sizes of type, which enabled different types to be used together easily. And also: the possibility of casting type on different sizes of body, so that an image could be set with different line increments. There was the invention of italics to work together with roman fonts, the development of small capitals, and the spread of roman itself. It seems that in the 350 years that followed there was expansion and technical improvement in paths that had already been laid. In the last 100 years, technique has added much to efficiency, speed, and control. But has much changed in essentials?

As regards the essential part of type design – defining and producing letter shapes – gravers and steel were the equal of present day high-end equipment. Of course we now have great advantages in positioning, repeating and generally controlling letters. We can do all of this faster and cheaper. And that is indeed important.

So the development and production of a typeface can be done quickly now. But what about the time it takes to design the character set of a classical roman? Or, more precisely, the time it took to make a set of punches in the sixteenth century, and the time it takes now to produce a set of outlines with weight variations. My risky guess is that the difference in time between doing the job then and doing it now is not so great. If one is thinking of upper- and lowercase, a set of numerals, punctuation marks and a few further essential characters, nowadays we might do it in not more than two weeks. A sixteenth-century punchcutter would need at least a month. But what if we want to make a complete typeface: all the necessary characters, a matching italic, small capitals, one or perhaps two further weights, and for all these characters to be able to work at all sizes. Then we may need another year or perhaps two. In the sixteenth century, something comparable – without the variations of weight – might take a year and a half. So any difference here, between then and now, is not great. Design time is not where the changes have occurred.

To design a whole font of a typeface, skill based in experience is always needed. Technology can help; but no more than help. It enables us to gain experience faster and cheaper, with more control, and more on our own terms – compared to other, older techniques. All this sounds good, and it is the blessing provided by what we have now. But these new freedoms are useless on their own. They become powerful when they are working together with something that provides a strong, clear directing lead: skill, knowledge, and experience. These are not magic ingredients that solve everything. They can even be a hindrance, preventing fresh thought. Freedoms are good, as long as you don't drown in the euphoria they seem to offer.

Another benefit of present technology is the tools or design software that we use. For centuries, the process used to be divided into three stages: designing characters (making punches); justifying characters (justification of matrices); casting type. These were three quite distinct, laborious tasks. But now, for the first time, the three jobs have been brought together by this software. The processes of defining a letterform, of allocating a width, of making and checking its final form – all happen in one go. You can switch between these tasks at any time. This flexibility has been possible since the mid-1980s. It really is something new, unthought of even in the days of advanced photocomposition, and which we owe to the software engineers of font-design programs. Is there a downside to this new freedom? An unavoidable clarity in the process has been lost: the distinct steps that the material forced on the designer. Designers now have to define their own steps.

For typeface designers, looking at the quality of their work in progress, no technology has fully been able to solve the question 'how will these characters look when used, when printed?' There is a striking difference between the punch and the character in print. We might say 'what runs out of a high-resolution image-setter matches the printed result better than a punch can match a letterpress-printed sheet'. But this is less true than it seems, given the striking difference between the sharp images on the smooth paper or film of the image-setter and the much rougher product of print. Punchcutters gave their characters relatively high contrast between thin and thick strokes. They knew that forms would fatten up in print. This could be imitated and anticipated, not by making smoke-proofs, which gave a true image only of the punch itself, but by inking the punch and impressing it into damp paper. In other words, they could test their products immediately under the conditions of letterpress printing.

Printing, or the actual production of text, is not so simple now as in the days of hand-operated letterpress. Type used to be a thing: a solid and predictable object. Today it is not solid, and the type designer cannot know how it will be used. The medium that carries the image may not be paper. Sizes are no longer standard or predictable [23.1]. And the designer no longer has the final say on how the type will be treated: on its design. This is strange. In the letterpress days we wanted delicate control over the shapes of the letters.

Now type designers have that. With the remarkable progress in offset lithography of the past thirty or so years, we expect type to be printed with great fidelity. But we type designers are losing all control over type in use. Again, our proud new freedom has to be qualified.

23.1

The designer of these letters did not imagine them reproduced at such a scale: the words 'let's play' are set in Denda New, a bespoke typeface designed by the author for Canon-Europe. (Antwerp, 2008.)

24 Type design and language

A huge amount has now been written about legibility. The literature ranges from empirical research conducted by psychologists to the more informal speculations of typographers. The latter will include discussion of word-spaces – smaller or larger? – or space between lines – 1 point more or less? These may be just details for the lay person, but for the typographer they are all-important factors in legibility and reading-comfort, and rightly so. As typographic technology has developed, we begin to talk not just about 1 point differences, but rather differences of 0.1 or 0.05 points. Such differences do have an effect; and it is all done in the service of the reader.

The typographer's play with numbers and fine tuning of details is attractive – too attractive. If you stop and think back to first principles, you will find another area that may affect readability as much as, if not more than, these typesetting variables. This is the way in which a particular language interacts with a particular typeface design. It is an almost undiscussed and unrecognized issue. Consider, for example, why it should be that French text looks so different from Dutch, or Dutch from English. Why does Irish text always look so nasty? What could be done to improve that?

In Latin text these visual awkwardnesses do not occur. The modern languages derived from Latin are also relatively free of unpleasantness in the text-image. Type specimens set in Latin may look beautiful, but they are useless for the typographer working in any modern language. And all this provides us with an explanation of the visual awkwardness of some languages.

The letterforms that became standard in formal writing and later in early printing were designed for the language they had to transmit, which was always Latin. Letter frequency and above all letter combination are the characteristics that determine the look of a language. So in writing – a highly flexible system of design and production – the forms of letters were determined by the frequency and combination characteristics of Latin: like stones being shaped by the movement of a water current. If Latin had had more use for the lowercase j, then this character would not hang from the x-line as it does, but rather stand on the baseline like n or float like o. The letter j is unique in this; and it is a historical mistake. But languages such as Dutch and English have to deal with it.

For reasons of standardization and blind obedience to efficiency and economics, typography has not looked further than a b c d e f g h i j k l m n o p q r s t u v w x y z. Dogmatic rules, and the wish to make a product that can serve all of us in every situation, have led us away from the real goals of legibility and readability. Strange things have happened in the history of languages and cultures, and one sees their residues in characters such as ß, æ, œ. Some languages hang on to them; but they could be replaced by alternative forms that would fit better.

We have 26 letters. How many words can you make with these 26 letters? Many: one can be sure about that. In considering the visual characteristics of a language, we do not usually get much further than saying that a certain character is used more in this language than in that one. Or we sometimes get more exact. We know that in 10,000 characters of average Dutch text, there will be 1586 e's, 1425 word-spaces and 858 n's.* But what do these numbers really say? You might reply that languages can be compared with each other. It may be that the letter y occurs two or three times more in English than in Dutch, and so on. To get the real information, one has to take a few steps further.

We know that we have 26 letters and that the number of words that can be made with them is beyond human calculation. However, if one considers all the possible letter combinations, then the number of shapes between these 26 letters can be counted: less than 150 for roman (lowercase and capitals), about 110 for italic. The letter x may not look strange to us, but xx does, certainly within a word: it does

* Battus, *Opperlandse taal- & letterkunde*, Amsterdam: Querido, 1981, p.123.

not seem possible, except in roman numerals. What is hard to accept is not the appearance of two x's, but the lozenge shape created by putting two x's next to each other [24.1]. Welsh, Friesian, and Irish are examples of languages that contain many of these unhappy combinations. These visual awkwardnesses tend to make a language look especially forbidding to learn and read. They suggest that the language has a weak written tradition, and a stronger spoken life. If these languages had been written down sufficiently over the centuries, then they would have acquired a visual quality of their own. But now, put abruptly into their ill-fitting typographic dress, they look odd.

Welsh, Irish, Friesian, Turkish, Finnish, Faroese, Malagasy.... What do I have to do with these languages? Nothing. If I were Welsh, then I could do something with typefaces for Welsh. But I wouldn't, because it is not worthwhile – or not worthwhile in the way that typography operates now. My mother-tongue is Dutch, and so I am more concerned with this silly j character, which crops up frequently

hot   not

24.1
The English language may use just 26 lowercase letters, but the number of ways in which they can be combined is huge. The shapes made by the space between these letters are however much fewer in number. Each letter must have its own form, but some right and left profiles are shared between several letters. Consider q and d, or n and h. Thus 'hot' and 'not' are two different words, but use the same shapes between the letters.

schrijn
schrijn
schrijn

schrijn

24.2

The problem of the lower case j that seems to hang (top, Romanée) is given an extreme solution in this early typeface by the author (middle). The serif at base-line level gives firm support to the character. Another treatment that follows this line of thinking can be seen in Scala (below).

in our language. It is 'silly' because it is better suited to Arabic than to typography in the Latin alphabet, where it hangs like a wet sock on a washing-line. Capital J can be made slightly more acceptable, just by putting it on the baseline. It then creates a hole on the left side, but only when it occurs in a word set all in capitals; though they should be spaced anyway. But the lowercase j is a big problem. Some designers try the remedy of giving it a corner to the right side of the lower part, so that it gets some support [24.2]. One can also add a little serif, on the baseline, so that it really has a foot to stand on. This also brings the right side more into relation with the forms of the other characters. Show some text using such a j to a graphic designer. In 12 point there will be no reaction: they just read it. But make it display size, and they start to groan. Ordinary people do not see the difference at any size, unless you point it out to them. A good solution probably lies somewhere in the middle.

 Experiments like these do offer a way of getting to grips with the characteristics and peculiarities of different languages. This may be so, even in designing for a language that one cannot read. And I think that investigation of these issues is more valuable than making another pleasant booklet about ampersands.

The relation between typography and language is not simple. Typography does not simply serve language. Typography can be seen as a threat to languages and cultures. We can even see typography as a serial killer of minor languages. Of course, 'typography' here cannot be separated from the larger forces of which it is part. So, on the one hand, typography seems to bring emancipation and openness, as it becomes available to everyone at reducing costs. While, at the same time, typography seems to say: 'if you can't keep up with the new developments, or if you don't fit into the pattern of reducing costs, then you will die'. There is a self-fulfilling prophecy here, which is founded on a narrow view of what is economic (though in recent years Microsoft has begun to provide for minority languages and scripts). Languages and cultures die off in the advance of Western civilization. Whatever view we take of this, it is happening. We should certainly regret that we let it happen without much conscious choice. Remedies would have to start with young people, in secondary-school classes. Along with music and art, we could teach skills in making and using letters.

25 The limits of roman

Enormous energy and effort have been put into type design and typography. Crudely put, it all boils down to this: the development and spread of roman letterforms, as printed and otherwise disseminated in a flood of documents throughout the Western world.

It all started with just a set of punches: a complete alphabet (and associated marks) cut on steel bars – a typeface. This basic set of letters was then expanded with a matching italic, with sloping capitals, with small capitals. Much effort was needed to do this well, so that the different components sat well together. Then attempts began to be made to give these fonts a common appearance over different sizes. And then the idea of a consistent design was consciously worked out and proposed (most clearly in the 'romain du roi'). This idea was then taken further with matching condensed and slightly bolder letters (was this what Fournier was trying to realize?). Meanwhile, type was not timeless. Fashion and changes in taste influenced it. The job had to be done all over again, with other stylistic features, by Bodoni and others. By the end of the eighteenth century, commercial pressures were beginning to become evident in type. The rise of display type, with endless variations of form, had started. Such letters had only a limited relation to type for continuous reading.

In the second half of the nineteenth century, typefoundries first began to reuse older matrices, and later made revivals of earlier forms: the term 'old style' originates there. With mechanization of type production, and powered typesetting and printing, the effects of such developments were widely felt. These revivals, which mostly took models from the first 150 years of printing with movable type, were not only made for use in plain reading matter, but were also elaborated and developed for application in printing that had no more than a commercial goal. So text typefaces were fattened and enlarged, to look like display types – with unsatisfactory results. And the notion of a typeface had begun to change.

By the early 1920s, a typeface was becoming a big project:
a family of letters that hoped to perform any task, at any size, in any
weight or width. The most successful of these typefaces are of course
those whose forms are best suited to this kind of treatment: sanserif
typefaces such as News Gothic and Franklin Gothic, Futura, and, later
on, Univers and Helvetica. The typographic roman was now a slow
and therefore expensive thing to make, which had to perform tasks
that are very difficult to achieve with just one design. This contrasts
strangely with the German goldsmiths at the end of the fifteenth
century, who were able to supply their Italian customers with new
designs that had taken less than a year to make. The idea of the all-
purpose typeface family began to sprawl, with further weights and
variations added, with imitation between competitors, and the pressure to provide at least as much of the same stuff as your competitors
were offering. It led to manufacturing firms with huge libraries
of typefaces.

As well as this race of competition to perform an impossible
task, there was, from the 1960s onwards, constant technical change.
Photocomposition, replacing metal composition, was soon followed
by digital techniques. The growth of roman and its influence did not
stop. War-horse typefaces such as Times Roman and Helvetica were
augmented with diacritical marks and special characters. Other ('non-
Latin') scripts were romanized in the style of these typefaces, to create
an even more extensive design, trading under just one name. Huge
character sets resulted. All of this was done with an eye to quality:
a goal that was and is important in this trade. But although the name
of quality was spoken, in fact it was sometimes passed over – for the
sake of efficiency, speed, and price.

When digital technology arrived it brought the frustrations that
every new technology carries with it. But with time and effort, we began to find new and previously unimagined levels of control. Quality
and control are good friends. In industrial processes they are more or
less twins.

25.1

The idea of infinitely modifiable type is not so new, and its 'invention' can hardly be attributed to one person. Gerrit Noordzij's approach to letters, in development over forty years, shows the potential of this approach. The two axes of 'translation' (as if produced by a broad-nibbed pen) and 'expansion' (a pen with flexing nib) are here given a third dimension.

174

So some early digital ideas were realized in everyday software of the late 1980s. For example, hinting and interpolation were thought about in the early 1970s – and are now taken for granted, as simply indispensable [25.1, 25.2]. They seem to give us back ways of handling type that we got used to in the days of metal, earlier in that century.

Such things are almost entirely in the hands of the type and software industry, and they take place behind curtains. To do things well still needs quite a large investment: it takes time, and requires knowledge and expertise. This still counts for formal type designs, and especially when they have to meet the requirements of spreadsheets, web-pages, databases, and interfaces in general. The problems that formal typography encounters today can be more complex and difficult than ever before. In this respect it seems that not much has changed. To get type working well still requires much effort.

Many people may dispute this. And, of course, there have been changes. Yes: many changes over the last thirty years, and they have not stopped yet. Typeface production is now open to the designers themselves. They have become a part of the type industry, and are no longer wallflowers waiting to be asked; and in the case of some designers, they have indeed become the industry itself.

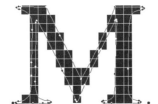 

25.2

The need for firm control over digital type encouraged complicated 'hinting' methods. With the application of hints, an outline is modified to adapt itself to the constraints of the raster, so as to produce an optimal visual representation.

175

This, together with the possibilities available within the new methods, is providing new paths for designers to take [25.3]. It all offers much more than we may realize at first sight. Such speculations are taken up in the next chapter.

Q   Q

QBE	Query-By-Example		QBE	Query-By-Example
QC	Quality Control		QC	Quality Control
QIC	Quarter-Inch-Cartridge		QIC	Quarter-Inch-Cartridge
QIS	QuickDraw Interchange Format		QIS	QuickDraw Interchange Format
QPS	Quark Publishing System		QPS	Quark Publishing System
QSAM	Queued Sequential Access Method		QSAM	Queued Sequential Access Method
QSP	QuickDraw Streaming Protocol		QSP	QuickDraw Streaming Protocol
QTAM	Queued Telecommunication Access Method		QTAM	Queued Telecommunication Access Meth
QUIC	Quadra Universal Interface Connector		QUIC	Quadra Universal Interface Connector

25.3

Variation on a page from a small book of computer acronyms, compiled and designed by Amy Ramsey. Although there may be just one typeface here (Kosmik), it is put to use in essentially different ways. On the left, the typeface is applied conventionally. On the right, it is allowed to 'flipper': shapes of letters vary on each occurrence, so they adopt different angles and positions. Look down the line of Q's. This might look like mere play, but 'scanability' and pleasure in reading may be enhanced by the variations. Such experiments (this one dates from the mid-1990s) could have their uses in very formal typography too and are easily possible with present-day techniques.

26 Openings and changes

Type design is still in the hands of specialists. With love they devote much time to forms, to space, and to what happens when these forms are greatly reduced in size. A historical view helps here.

When typefoundries were established in the seventeenth century, this was the beginning of the slow process by which punchcutters became just executors of someone else's designs. Later, at the end of the nineteenth century, with the introduction of the pantograph into type production, the punchcutter disappeared altogether. Much time and effort was then necessarily put into developing and articulating experience. This experience consisted mainly in making a bridge between the design (the working drawings) and what happened when text was set and printed in its final small sizes. But 'design' really means not just working drawings, but justification and reduction of the letters. What is a designer doing if the last two parts are missing from the design process? Just muddling around? Justification and reduction were usually in the hands of production people, and some-times the first stage of working drawings was in their hands too. It was only after some years of time- and money-consuming experiment that a designer, by then working on further typefaces, could even begin to see what he was doing.

A few designers in the industrial period – W. A. Dwiggins is a no-table example – had good, mutually trusting relationships with produc-tion people. They developed a way of working that brought producer and designer close together, without losing the ability to change and steer the forms, in agreed ways. Dwiggins made stencil shapes in sizes that were as small as possible, but yet large enough for him to have control over them.

However, most type designers of the industrial era seem to have been shortsighted and timorous people. They kept whatever know-ledge they had to themselves. And they regarded production not as an essential constituent of design, but as a necessary evil, on a lower intellectual level. The designer's long journey towards a state of sufficient experience was quite an investment. This investment had to be jealously guarded. These men took great care to present themselves as a special breed, not much influenced by anything outside typography: a small circle of people for a small market. Dressed in suits and drinking fine wine, they may have talked about letters, written essays about their own and each other's typefaces. But the transfer of knowledge was not their aim. This, more or less, is the impression one gets of the famous type designers of the first half of the twentieth century.

There is no place for such attitudes now. Try them and see where you get. A true advantage of present-day conditions is that production of typefaces can be implemented quicker than ever before and under your own control. What you make today is tested tomorrow, in any size you want. And what, forty years ago, took months to do can now be done in a few days. So you can learn from what you have done much quicker than ever before.

But it is not as simple and easy as this implies. A designer must still have something to say. There has to be a good reason to design yet another typeface. This reason can be fed – created – by everyday practice. You do not design a typeface just like that. First you must have some acquaintance with the existing typefaces, preferably by using them. Only then will you be able to see what is needed, and be able to specify your wishes adequately, so as to provide what apparently doesn't yet exist. Then begins the period of making, of testing visual quality, and of testing how it really works in use. All this takes time. The things that really count in the process of testing are human factors; they don't have much to do with technique. These human considerations will never change as quickly as technique itself. To achieve something in type design – I am referring to long-term, continuous-text typography – one needs experience; and gaining this experience still takes five to ten years, at least.

There is enough reason to assume that talented young designers learn very quickly. This is not only due to new techniques – computers – but also because of the fact that in a few places experience is

well absorbed and communicated in a very effective way. A number
of type-design courses have come to the fore – especially those at The
Hague, Reading, and Leipzig. At each of these places the educational
practice shows a continuity with typography before the digital era;
tradition can be investigated in a lively way. This continuity has been
helped by the fact that each of them is a public institution and has
thus been able to plan for the longer term.

The need for printed matter is still growing. So there is more
opportunity to gain experience. Technical development does help.
But when you come to consider carefully, it helps less than we first assume. Educational institutions and technical facilities can do no more
than provide the circumstances in which young designers have the
chance to learn for themselves. As long as people are the creators and
users of type, the true limits will be human not technical.

One of these limits or conditioning factors is age. Young designers are also young human beings: they have all the advantages and the
disadvantages of being young. Some mistakes have to be made over
and over again. But the technical developments of the last few years
have cleared the way for young type designers: this cannot be denied.
The average age of the type designer has dropped astonishingly. These
are not just the celebrated young Dutch, but also French, Germans,
Americans – and more.

New techniques always influence young people faster than they
do older ones. The young ones grow up with it; they don't have to
transfer from something earlier. Technology, young practitioners,
many social changes – all this has meant that the gate for small-scale
diversity has been opened. Whether this also means that these new
possibilities are going to be used fruitfully is hard to know. These are
times without rules, without strong social movements or ideologies
that can generate clear attitudes or beliefs. Everybody can do what
they want; every attitude or style has its place. So judgement is difficult, and we are thrown back to human essentials: the constraints
of the human body, of human perception, of usability.

The famous 'first principles' of Stanley Morison may not be

nonsense now, but they are not quite true either. The idea that 'type design moves at the pace of the most conservative reader' is just fantasy.* People produce text in the ways that they want and need. They certainly do not wait for Stanley. The more diversity the better. If teenage television uses irregular and shaky all-capital subtitles, then which inky typographer has the right to say that it is no good? Nobody – except for me, who was once interested in one of their programmes. I wanted to read the subtitles of an interview, but just couldn't keep up with them. And neither could most of my students, who belong to its target-group. You can go too far, even now. If you want people to really read something, then do not use type as illustration.

The traditionalists or, better, the conventional dogmatists are often offended by new technologies. Certainly they are if these technologies seem to encourage disrespect for rules and conventions. But every coin has two sides. Apart from moaning, the conventional people have not yet done much with the possibilities provided by this technology, which in fact might fit well with their conventional ideas. They cannot make this adjustment, because there are still too many flowers placed at the ivory tower of typography. Standing guard above its entrance are statues of Morison-like deities. The aura of these men (no women among them) is still too powerful. We should remove these statues without delay. Then, the ivory tower and its mystique will collapse.

The statues do not need to be blown up, only removed to the department of book typography. This needs to be seen for what it is: just one among several departments of typography. It is a strange place: the only one with statues. Why do we see statues in our mind as soon as we start to talk about book or long-term typography? Names – statues – loom up: Morison, Van Krimpen, Gill, Tschichold ...

* Stanley Morison, *First principles of typography*, Cambridge: Cambridge University Press, 1967, p. 7.

And then? Enough people complain that students of graphic design know hardly anything about history. Is that so bad? Does knowledge of Morison really help them? What does he really say to our students? Nothing: because he never said anything to any twenty-year old, whether digital or not. But we can't blame it all on Stanley Morison. It is we later typographers who have been trying to make his stone image speak. We have tended to look only at the products and the dogmas, and not at the processes and the questions behind them. The students' 'Stanley who?' is not the point. If they are interested and serious, then they will meet up with him.

We could better spend time in encouraging students to be honest. Only honest designers can look freshly at the new challenges (fresh does not mean wild). Only honest designers can chuck out the typographic sludge and see what is left. And then they can decide what is worth adding to the typographic repertoire. 'Worthwhile' is hard to define, because even in book typography the borders are open. Why, for example, should one use some third- or fourth-hand Baskerville imitation, which doesn't begin to work visually, just for the sake of the statue named 'Baskerville'?

Apart from the matter of typeface style, there is the question of what we might need in the way of special symbols or 'sorts' that have to sit in text. Technology has made it possible to specify your own typographic material: not just letterforms but anything that you may want to put under a key-stroke. Many designers still do not realize what this means. This is sad, because new typographic material and new procedures cannot come just from type designers. There are potential contributors among users of all kinds. And one of the great advantages of the digital era is the fact that these users can make or specify their own typographic materials. We can only be glad that programs that allow this have been written and are easily available.

There is nothing to stop us from keeping what is good and even expanding on it. There is nothing to prevent typography from developing further – in serious ways – not least in all those departments that don't share much with traditional book design. There are still wide-open, almost undiscovered areas: especially in information design, and in all the other fields that are not exclusively based in printing on paper.

One area of explosive growth is in digital products and online services that use or are built around graphic interfaces. And there is no reason to think that this is just a temporary phenomenon. A number of design disciplines are of essential importance here, among them screen typography. Type designers need to work in close collaboration with other specialists, on user interfaces and in other related fields. This has to be so in order to create efficient and product-specific solutions. Because the market is notably global in character, support for non-Western languages and non-Latin scripts is a pressing concern. (Since the first edition of this book, 1996, work in these areas has developed remarkably.)

Despite the futuristic scenario (online connections around the globe, via civil satellites), the technology that the screen designer faces is rather bare and primitive. Low-resolution television monitors are being pressed into use to display complex information. The type designer may again be faced with an x-height of 6 pixels. This brings us back to the start of the book: the very basic question of how to make an acceptable word-image (chapter 4). The familiar medium of paper tends to be rather forgiving: in our perception of it, and in its resolution of images and text. By comparison screens are harsh in both respects, though we accept low resolution in images much more easily than in text.

These new developments are mainly taking place in the privileged and educated parts of the world. The resources of typography tend to be channelled into a rather narrow sector – of computer companies, design education, specialized journals. The empire of technically advanced typography feeds too much on itself and provides its own justifications, without connection to the rest of the societies in which it operates.

Meanwhile, a large part of the Western world manages well enough without design. Go into a shopping centre in any town, and look at the signs announcing 'sale': they will be off-the-peg notices, used by jewellers as well as clothes shops. The antique shop owner puts an old chair outside the shop, with a clumsy 'open' sign on the seat (so clumsy, that you feel a bit jealous). Any Japanese tourist walking by knows at once exactly what is going on here. No 'design' can ever beat this. 'Quality' – whatever this is – is not wanted here, unless it's for free. What is wanted is something quick and cheap. This will never change.

We designers are working more for ourselves – typography for typographers – than we like to admit or, even less, to contemplate. There is a world going on outside where we are not wanted, and where we couldn't help anyway. Typography still has an aura of good intentions attached to it: 'clarity', 'readability', 'communication', and all the other words to which people nod 'yes'.

All the technical changes have enabled this significant social fact: that access to type is open to a much larger number of people than was the case even twenty years ago. The grip of the large manufacturers has been loosened. Typographic material can be produced with significantly less production time, labour, and capital; the risks involved are much smaller. It is easy to try experiments, to repeat and learn from them. There is an open path for younger or more radical designers to create a climate in which preconceptions, habits, rites, and dogmas can be questioned or just disregarded. Typography has become a stage on which young designers have dared to put on a fool's mask, to play the role of clown. At first the results were amusing, sometimes challenging. But this coin has two sides, and by now the stage is rather crowded with people wearing these masks, imagining masks to be real faces. But currents like these have certainly loosened up the whole typographic scene. The established type manufacturers have simply had to accept this, along with other much bigger forces such as financial pressure and corporate rationalization. They have adapted, or have been absorbed into one another, or have disappeared.

It was in the nature of type (and its printed applications) to have a formal character – simply because it took time, knowledge, and capital. It was and is an investment, and one that you do not fool around with. People want to make use of their investments for as long they can. So type design was very formal, and type had to endure the storms of time for as long as possible. It is not surprising that in the first three hundred years of printing only formal and semi-formal types were made.

The inverse is also true. Nowadays type can be bought cheap, simply because often it does not take much knowledge, labour, or capital to make it (especially when you pirate an existing product). It is generally accepted that what is got easily is not of much value. No harm is done if these easily won goods have a short life and an unsure future. Not much escapes from this principle. Seen like this, the explosive growth of fun type is no more than logical.

The screen has become an important carrier of information. But it is not going to replace anything, it is simply an addition to all the carriers we already have. Trying to understand screens is an almost impossible business. They are a generally accepted phenomenon, but one that is hardly 50 years old. When thinking about text typography, which originated on paper (or similar substrates), we do not do much more than compare screens with pieces of paper. Then the result is rather frustrating. But the screen is nothing like a piece of paper. And if I say 'screen', what exactly do I mean? To answer this question correctly is beyond the scope of this book. Let's say that a screen is simply anything that can carry information and which is able to refresh itself. It does not matter whether this happens by means of rays, pixels, or cubes that turn around. It is the ability to refresh a display with different content (which can't be done with this book) that makes the screen so important. This also means that we are able to get text and images to move around or change colour. In short, we are able to treat information as animation. This is a powerful design tool and for typography it really is something new. Apart from some early Bauhaus experiments and some cartoons, not very much work has been done to explore these possibilities. As far as I know there is not even a proper book (!) about it. But now screen-based or animated typography is

184

being put to work in the exploding world of graphic interfaces, web-sites, and related areas. How this will influence type design and typo-graphy is hard to know. What is exciting is the fact that there is not much history to go back to. With Gutenberg's 'movable' type we refer to something essentially different, and not very helpful as a comparison.

The transformation of type from a fixed, material embodiment into a digital file opens up further possibilities. Typefaces can be smart. They can be made to modify and change appearance at random [25.3]. This is just the start of the new potentials. Smart typefaces will be able to do much more than simply represent themselves; and whatever they might do it won't stop at screens. Again, it is rather an open field, with unknown horizons. It should go without saying that these open areas, full of possibility, are transparent. They do not belong to a specific style, or movement, or use.

What all this means for type design and typography is that the new things are not computers, pixels, béziers, or the internet. The really new things are cheapness, decrease in formality, animation, and built-in intelligence. This is how it looks now. Type design, and ty-pography more generally, continues to grow. It can be rather complex: so big and complex that it escapes our grasp. Expertise is needed more than ever. But whatever happens, it happens around us and not within us. Nothing can make my eye scan better than it does already, or make your brain more sensitive to tonal values. These are the foundations, and they do not change.

––––––––

We might think that much has happened since this book was first pub-lished, fifteen years ago. Yes, there have been some changes, but hardly any fundamental progress has been made. Laser printers have a resolu-tion of 600 dpi as standard, and they might print colour too. Our LCD screens have colour and grey values – very helpful for displaying type acceptably at reading sizes, and photorealistic images look even better. Resolutions only increase, together with the physical size of the screen. At the same time screens are shrinking: portable mini-screens seem to serve our needs wherever we go.

Non-Latin scripts are now treated seriously, not just from an academic point of view, but also as a field for everyday design. This was fed on one side by a technical development – the acceptance of OpenType as a standard font format, which enabled us to display scripts more complex than plain Latin. From another side, non-Latins were taken up by the discipline of type design (the course at Reading has played a leading role here). Online global communication has become normal: screen type must now outrun printed type, although the use of paper still grows. The rift between those connected 24 hours a day, and those who fall behind, becomes a synonym for the rich and the poor. The poor: thirsty for knowledge; the rich: filling their time, sharpening their social abilities in a virtual way. Harmless as this seems, it is decadent, if you think what two or three laptops might mean for the youth of a village somewhere in Africa.

Nevertheless, whether on screen or printed, it should all ideally be done with one and the same font file. Current problems are again solved on the wrong side: the side of type. If all browsers were to make use of the same rasterizer, a typeface would be treated the same no matter what browser is employed. The world – the user – certainly does not need another big font problem.

Meanwhile the stage (p.183) has become overcrowded: so crowded that virtual stages are a welcome solution. Anyone who cannot perform in the real world is offered a second chance. Alas, letting everyone have his or her say has its price. The idea of being heard is an attractive one, so attractive that we start to believe that this in itself is more important than what is being said. Type design as a discipline did not escape from this vulgarity and all that comes with it.

And, last but not least, we still do not have real animated type! By this I do not mean a movie in which some letters start to move around. No, we are waiting for font files that have built within them the capacity to animate. Technically this is possible today, but it will still take some time before animated type, at least as a simple and optional effect, is a common design tool.

Appendices

Hendrik van den Keere

Henric vanden keere de Ionghe | Lettersteker | wenscht allen bemind-
ers van goeden Letteren | in alles voorderinghe ende verstant met God.
Eersame ende lieve Leser | aenghesien datter alreede vele ende ver-
scheyden gheschreven Letteren by Drvcke int licht ghecomen zijn |
zo tot voorderinghe vander Ioncheyt | als ooc eensdeels wt nie-
wicheyt: zo hebben wy ons ooc met den anderen dorren bestaen (niet
wt verwaende vermetelheyt dat kendt God | nemaer alleenlijc tot ex-
ercitie ende wt liefden der Consten) ooc een ander niev gheschreven
Letter int licht te brijnghen | waer af wy V. L. met desen een proefken
presenteren | na die gracye die ons God ghegheven heeft. Bidden V. L.
tzelve over danckelijc t'accepteren | verhopend beters metter tijt |
by der hvlpen Gods | wiens ghenade wy v bevelen.

Henric vanden keere the younger | letter-cutter | wishes divine
furtherance and favour in all things | to all lovers of good type.
Honoured and beloved reader | seeing that many and various script
types have by now appeared in print | made for the benefit of youth |
and partly for novelty: we (not out of pride or presumption, God
knows | but in the ordinary exercise of our art and for the love of
it) have seen fit to produce another | and hereby we lay before you a
small specimen of it | as God has given us grace. We beg you to accept
it | and meanwhile we hope to do better | with God's help | and pray
His blessing upon you.

This is the text reproduced in our illustration 3.7 (p. 23). The transcription
was made by Alexander Verberne. The translation into English is adapted
from that given in: Harry Carter & H. D. L. Vervliet, *Civilité types*, Oxford:
Oxford Bibliographical Society, 1966.

188

Renard

ne futorem quidem ar

The text of this book uses a new typeface, Renard, designed by the author and issued by The Enschedé Font Foundry. Renard has the forms of the 'Dutch' roman ('le goût Hollandois' that Fournier wrote about disparagingly). The letters – lowercase and associated capitals – follow Hendrik van den Keere's 2-line Double Pica Roman (Gros Canon), cut around 1570 and shown in Plantin's folio specimen of c.1585 [A.1 above]. This was a large letter, for use in choir books and in display setting. It is rather condensed, with proportionately large x-height, and dark in colour. To purist eyes, some of the characters might seem out of balance with each other: but in text they work together happily and with assurance. Van den Keere never cut a complete italic, so Renard's italic is a new design, made in the spirit of the period. In designing Renard, Van den Keere's punches for the type were inspected – along with its early printed appearances. Two of them are shown on the title pages of this book.

Renard captures the elusive, off-balance quality of its model: thus the name. Although broadly in the category of Garamond, it makes a fresh contribution. Deviating from current thinking about typefaces, it is limited in its style variants. Already black in colour, it has no 'bold'. Rather, two lighter weights are provided, to supplement the weight used here. A set of titling capitals will be added.

This note on the typeface Renard was included in the first edition of the book. We reproduce the text here unchanged and still set in Renard, although this book is otherwise now set in the typeface Haultin. The two punches mentioned are not now shown on the book's title pages, and the set of Renard titling capitals has not yet been added.

Haultin

Pierre Haultin (1510/13–1587/8), a contemporary of both Claude Garamond (1510/13–1561) and Robert Granjon (1510/13–1590) can easily
be considered the equal of those two punchcutters. And these three,
together with Antoine Augerau, Simon de Colines, and Guillaume Le
Bé I stand together at the top of a small group of French punchcutters
whose names and work still enjoy some fame even today.

In comparison with Garamond and Granjon, Haultin seems to
be the most complete practitioner. He was not just a punchcutter. He
managed casting projects, as well as the printing of quite a few books.
If the right typeface was not available, Haultin simply cut it. He was
also a copper-plate engraver and woodcutter. All this he did on his
own account or in the service of well-known printing houses, such as
that of Robert Estienne I.

A name such as Robert Granjon comes down to us mainly because of his thirst for experiment and his vivid style within the art of
punchcutting for type – and therefore the role he played within that
world. By contrast, Pierre Haultin represents much more a position
in which the punchcutter's skills are used for a specific movement or
attitude within printing. As H. D. L. Vervliet wrote: 'At the cradle of
the new Geneva typography for Bibles and Psalters there stood a simple craftsman: Pierre Haultin. The large and rapid expansion of the
Reformation in France coincides with the growth of the Geneva Bible
printing in the years 1550–60 ...'*

For type design this means that Haultin was perhaps not the
first but certainly among his contemporaries he was the most notable
creator of the cost-effective printed page of text (which made all those
cheap pocket bibles a reality). Haultin can be regarded as the godfather
of no-nonsense work-horse typefaces. He is the kind of man who,

---

* H. D. L. Vervliet, *The palaeotypography of the French Renaissance*, Leiden:
Brill, 2008, vol. I, p. 246.

even if something is already there, will still see reasons to improve it, just in order to save another line or two on the page (without sacrificing anything on legibility). This is an aim that recurred frequently in the centuries that followed.

Haultin's text letters first caught my attention through the facsimile of the Vatican specimen *Indice de caratteri* (1628). The narrowness of some of the Haultin fonts there was striking. Ever since then Haultin's types have haunted me. In the early 1990s I made photographic enlargements and started to compare them with my own Quadraat. I noticed that many Haultin fonts had even narrower counters than Quadraat, which is already very efficient. I thought I had done a good job with Quadraat but apparently Haultin was much more daring.

A striking feature of Haultin's types is his lowercase a which often falls to the right, often a bit too much; and this characteristic feature has been tempered in my interpretation. Another feature is the rather large top bowl of his lowercase g. These features are easily recognizable and let us identify his work.

His types were used widely and whenever I was looking at something printed in the sixteenth century or later there was a good chance that I might notice the use of a Haultin letter. By accident I came across them again and again, whether at some exhibition that contained old printed books, or in a television history film: the expert reads a passage from an old book and the camera shows a close-up of the printed text and, yes, a Haultin typeface! Haultin's types were widely appreciated and in use up to the start of the nineteenth century.

Although this was not his conscious aim, he moved among printers and intellectuals who were by nature critical and who were not afraid to doubt or even fight all that what was forbidden by the Catholic church. Many of his customers were free-thinkers and we can say that many titles that were considered seditious or at least suspect, because of their radical content, were indeed printed with Haultin types. One notable title is Galileo Galilei's *Siderius nuncius* (Venice 1610).

Some may consider this Haultin typeface to be a revival, but I would question that. With Renard there were punches, matrices, and

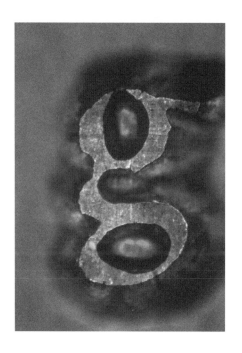

bitio & vulgi fauoris amor oếm
:quitatế & iuftitiã deprauant.ʒ 1
bitió ad quid cõcitauit duos fra-
:es & reliquos decế apoft.   100
bitio fons bellorum & diffidio-
um.   100
bitio tyrannica eft, & graui indi
ens reprehenfione.   75
bitio quid fecit in Romanis.100

printed material available. With Haultin there are no punches left; there are some matrices [A.2], and there is printed material [A.3]. But still you cannot call it a revival, because of the small size of the model. Renard, for example, was based on a letter with an x-height a little smaller than 7 millimetres: you can have a proper look at that. For Haultin I mainly looked at the matrices of the Coronelle Romaine and the Nonpareille Romaine (approximately 6.5 and 5.8 points). These are small sizes, but at least they give you a clear look at proportions. The ragged images found in the matrices are helpful but hardly represent how the letters came to us – deformed, or actually in this case touched up, by the printing process. Switching between the fixed image found in the matrices and the variety of images found in the printed result, the balance shifted in the end clearly towards the printed images. The margin for interpretation in a case like this is great. It is so large that, no matter who has done it, such a piece of work can only be called a personal interpretation.

A.2

The lowercase g from Haultin's Coronelle Romaine. This is the image left in the matrix by the punch (now lost).

A.3

A detail of a text printed with Haultin's Coronelle Romaine. Another sample of this printing is shown, at real size, in illustration 20.2 (p.139).

Literature

The essential works on punchcutting, as well as some of the more marginal items, are listed here.

F.C. Avis, *Edward Philip Prince: type punchcutter*, London: Avis, 1967
Harry Carter, *Fournier on typefounding: the text of the 'Manuel typographique' (1764–1766)*, London: Soncino Press, 1930
(reprint: New York: Franklin, 1973)
——, 'Optical scale in typefounding', *Typography*, no. 4, 1937
——, 'Letter design and typecutting', *Journal of the Royal Society of Arts*, vol. 102, 1954
——, 'Plantin's types and their makers', *De Gulden Passer*, vol. 37, 1956
——, 'The types of Christopher Plantin', *The Library*, 5th series, vol. 11, 1956
——, *A view of early typography up to about 1600*, Oxford: Clarendon Press, 1969 (reprint: London: Hyphen Press, 2002)
Benvenuto Cellini, *Treatises on goldsmithing and sculpture*, translated by C.R. Ashbee, London: Essex House Press, 1898
(reprint: New York: Dover Books, 1967)
Henk Drost, 'Punchcutting demonstration', *Visible Language*, vol. 19, no. 1, 1985
[Enschedé] *Proef van letteren:* facsimile of the Enschedé type specimens of 1768 & 1773, with a commentary by John Lane, 2 vols, Haarlem: Stichting Museum Enschedé, 1993
Pierre-Simon Fournier, *Manuel typographique* [1764 & 1766], ed. James Mosley, 3 vols, Darmstadt: Technische Hochschule Darmstadt, 1995
György Haiman, *Nicholas Kis: a Hungarian punchcutter and printer 1650–1702*, Budapest: Akadémia, 1983
Sem Hartz, 'An approach to designing type', in his *Essays*, Aartswoud: Spectatorpers, 1992

Frans A. Janssen, 'Ploos van Amstel's description of type founding',
   Quaerendo, vol. 20, no. 2, 1990
——, *Fleischman on punchcutting*, Aartswoud: Spectatorpers, 1994
Rudolf Koch, 'Vom Stempelschneiden', *Gutenberg Jahrbuch*, 1931
Jan van Krimpen, *A letter to Philip Hofer on certain problems connected
   with the mechanical cutting of punches*, Cambridge, Mass:
   Harvard College Library, 1972
Joseph Moxon, *Mechanick exercises on the whole art of printing* [1683],
   ed. Herbert Davis and Harry Carter, Oxford University Press,
   1958 (reprint: New York: Dover Books, 1978)
Stan Nelson, ' "Any fool can cut a punch..." ', *Matrix*, no. 4, 1984
Christian Paput, *La Gravure du poinçon typographique*, Massy:
   TVSO Éditions
Inventory of the Plantin-Moretus Museum: punches and matrices, Antwerp:
   Plantin-Moretus Museum, 1960
Rollo G. Silver, *Typefounding in America, 1787–1825*, Charlottesville:
   University Press of Virginia, 1965
Type specimen facsimiles 16–18: reproductions of Christopher Plantin's
   Index sive specimen characterum, 1567, and Folio specimen of
   c.1585, together with the Le Bé-Moretus specimen, c.1599,
   with annotations by H.D.L.Vervliet and Harry Carter,
   Toronto: University of Toronto Press, 1972
[Vatican Press] *Indice de caratteri*: facsimile of the Vatican Press,
   type specimen of 1628, with an introduction and notes by
   H.D.L.Vervliet, Amsterdam: Hertzberger, 1967
H.D.L.Vervliet, *Sixteenth-century printing types of the Low Countries*,
   Amsterdam: Hertzberger, 1968
——, *The palaeotypography of the French Renaissance: selected papers on
   sixteenth-century typefaces*, 2 vols, Leiden: Brill, 2008

Of the literature on the historical and cultural context of this topic,
Peter Burke's *The Renaissance* (London: Macmillan, 1987) is very helpful.

Illustration sources

Except where otherwise indicated, drawings and photographs are by the author. The photographs on pages 12, 42, 78, 144, 160, are from videos made by the author.

We are very grateful to the following colleagues for their help with illustrations:

Erik van Blokland provided fonts for 25.3

Jelle Bosma (Monotype Typography) provided a file for 25.2

Corina Cotorobai made this photograph: 23.1

Jonathan Hoefler provided a file for 3.8

Martin Majoor made the photograph of the author, used on the flap

Rob Mostert made these photographs: 9.1, 9.2, 12.1, 12.2, 12.3

Gerrit Noordzij provided film for 25.1

The electron microscope photographs, 12.4, 12.5, were made at Océ-Nederland

Erik Vos made these photographs: 3.7, 10.1, 10.3, 10.4, 20.1, 20.2, 20.3, 20.4

Pp. 12, 42, 78, 134, 144, 160, 192: Plantin-Moretus Museum, Antwerp

3.5   W. A. Dwiggins, US Linotype Caledonia specimen, 1939

3.6   Imre Reiner, *Grafika*, St Gallen: Zollikofer, 1947

3.7   Plantin-Moretus Museum, Antwerp [R 63.8]

6.1   Meermanno-Westreenianum Museum, The Hague [3F24]

6.3   Meermanno-Westreenianum Museum, The Hague [10D16]

6.4   Meermanno-Westreenianum Museum, The Hague [10C155]

6.6   British Museum, London [Harley 2577]

6.8   Meermanno-Westreenianum Museum, The Hague [2D22]

6.11   Jan Tschichold, *Letter kennis*, Mijdrecht: Stichting Graphilec, n.d.

7.1   The Newberry Library, Chicago

7.3   St Bride Library, London

7.4   St Bride Library, London

7.5   St Bride Library, London

7.6   St Bride Library, London

Illustration sources

7.7 St Bride Library, London
9.1 Centraal Museum Utrecht
10.1 Plantin-Moretus Museum, Antwerp [R 6.5]
10.2 Universiteitsbibliotheek Leiden [629 G 13:1]
10.3 Plantin-Moretus Museum, Antwerp [A 2007]
10.4 Plantin-Moretus Museum, Antwerp [A 1007]
10.5 André Jammes, *La Réforme de la typographie royale sous Louis XIV*, Paris: Paul Jammes, 1961
19.1 H.D.L. Vervliet, *Sixteenth-century printing types of the Low Countries*
20.1 Plantin-Moretus Museum, Antwerp [R 6.5]
20.2 Plantin-Moretus Museum, Antwerp [A 1813]
20.3 Plantin-Moretus Museum, Antwerp [A 415]
20.4 Plantin-Moretus Museum, Antwerp [A 146]
21.4 Stan Knight, *Historical scripts*, London: A. & C. Black, 1984
22.1 Jaques Saurin, *Sermons sur divers textes ...*, The Hague: Husson, 1715
22.2 Lewis Carroll, *Through the looking-glass and what Alice found there*, London: Macmillan, 1908
22.3 Stanley Morison, *Grondbeginselen van de typografie*, Utrecht: De Haan, 1951
22.4 Richard Rubenstein, *Digital typography*, Reading, Mass: Addison Wesley, 1988
A.1 H.D.L. Vervliet, *Sixteenth-century printing types of the Low Countries*
A.3 Plantin-Moretus Museum, Antwerp [A 1813]

The text used in the settings in 4.4 and 5.2–5.5 comes from a column ('Journey to the end of an alphabet') by Neal Ascherson in the *Independent on Sunday*, 7 November 1993.

For permission to reproduce material in their possession, as indicated above, grateful acknowledgement is made to: Plantin-Moretus Museum, Antwerp; The Newberry Library, Chicago; Meermanno-Westreenianum Museum, The Hague; Universiteitsbibliotheek Leiden; British Museum, London; St Bride Library, London; Centraal Museum Utrecht.

Index